WEST TO EAST AND BACK AGAIN

An Unusual Life and Time

HUDSON B. DRAKE

outskirts
press

"OUR LIMITS ARE NO LESS - THAN WE MAKE THEM"

Michael Schumacher

To Mary with love

Table of Contents

Preface

Why write this book? Good question!

As in so many important life decisions, my wife played an important and persistent role. Mary thought it would be a good idea to document the variety of people, places, and events that formed my life story. Encouraged by my family and a number of close friends, I embraced the idea of an autobiography; a chance to pass my life story on to my children and theirs.

When I began to consider the phases of my life, I was surprised by how much fun it was to remember people, times, and events. Of course, some portions were a great struggle. Unfortunately, over the years, family members died and scrap books were scattered. A lot of basic information on the family was lost and thus unavailable to me.

I worked in an exciting time in the aerospace, aeronautics, and electronics world. The mid 1950s into the 1990s were loaded with remarkable technological breakthroughs, and I was present for the convergence of material science, space flight, aeronautics, solid state electronics and advanced systems. Add in political climate and major shifts in defense procurement policies and you can begin to appreciate the magnitude of the changes going on in the industry, as well as the world. As is often the case in life, timing was critical... Fortunately, mine was mostly good.

I received great support from Geoff Shepard (White House Fellows), Charles Sparks (Teledyne Ryan Electronics), Tony Richards (Teledyne Ryan Aeronautical), Terry Lyons (Corporate life), and, Bill Tribolet, for an overview of the entire book. A special thanks to my editor, Brenda Taulbee, a delightful and talented young woman, and Lauri Anderson, who's computer skills were critical. My heartfelt thanks as well to the many men and women who contributed so much time and talent to the companies I led. All my success flowed through them.

I've written about the people and experiences that shaped my life and career with the sincere hope that some of the things I did (or didn't do) along the way, might help each reader in his or her own quest for excellence.

CHAPTER ONE

The Early Years:
1935 to 1957

FAMILY HISTORY

I came into the world a little after 6:00 p.m. on March 3, 1935 at Hollywood Presbyterian Hospital, on Sunset Blvd., in Los Angeles, California. My parents were Blossom Billings Drake, and Hudson Charles Drake.

I know from my folks that we lived on Hoover Ave. in Los Angeles for some years. I had a brother, Lee Allen Drake, "Lad," nine years older than I, and a sister, Cynthia Blossom Drake, "Cynthy," seven years older. My arrival was a bit of a surprise for my folks as they thought their family was complete! There were some old pictures of me being held by a black nanny named Ellen Young. More about her later.

My father was the first son of Theodora Merckle and Vivian Drake, born in Los Angeles on October 20, 1901. He had younger twin brothers, Theodore and Vivian. His mother was of Bavarian stock, and his father, English. His parents were a bit of a mystery to me. I know that his mother was from Illinois and her family were dairymen, with roots in Southern Germany. His dad was born in New Orleans and came to California in the late 1800s. Dad was a University of California graduate, and a member of the Alpha Tau Omega Fraternity. He was raised in Los Angeles, attended public schools, and played the trumpet.

Dad worked in Los Angeles at the Edison Building at 5th and steep Grand, for two companies; Belridge Oil, and Rodeo Land and Water. Belridge was a crude oil producer with a 31,000-acre field in the Lost Hills area, near the city of Taft, California. We used to drive up there through the Grapevine, which was always exciting when my dad was driving! The company sold crude oil to Shell and Union Oil who refined it. Belridge's field produced for over 100 years! The Rodeo Land and Water Company held over three thousand acres in the Los Angeles area which would develop into Beverly Hills, thus, Rodeo Drive.

My dad was a purchasing agent, though I suppose now he would be called a buyer. He was not athletic, due in part at least to an early head injury which ruled out any kind of contact sports. He worked hard, and suffered from nasty migraine headaches until he quit smoking, and then they just stopped. All three of us kids stayed well clear of dad when he had a headache. We could gauge his ap-proachability by the presence or absence of a vein pulsing in his forehead.

I'm not sure about the timing, I think in the late 40s or early 50s Dad got a raise to $1,000 a month and a company car. He and mom really celebrated. Years later he retired as executive vice president. Belridge was a privately owned company, and while my dad worked there for 45 years, he always counseled me to never work for a privately held company if you wanted a real career.

My mom, Blossom, was born in Long Island, New York on December 26, 1908. My grandfather, among other things, was a train conductor and also a carpenter. The family moved West in time for my mom to attend and graduate from Los Angeles High School, as did my dad. She later attended the Otis Art Institute there.

My brother, Lee (Lad) was born in Los Angeles on October 16, 1926. After being discharged from the Navy after the war, he went to the University of New Mexico and graduated with a degree in Mechanical Engineering in 1950. He was a member of the Sigma Chi Fraternity. Dad had introduced him to various leaders in the oil business over the years, and that was his industry of choice. He began his career as a store man at Continental Supply in Santa Fe Springs, California. His company merged and he moved to Texas in 1958, and later to Dallas, where he spent the bulk of his career. He was appointed President of the LTV Energy Company there in 1977, and named CEO in 1980. Lad was active in his community and his church, serving on the vestry and the Foundation of the St. Michael and All Angels Episcopal Church. He died of undiagnosed prostate cancer in August of 1986 at the age of 59. He is survived by his wife, Eleanor Greer Drake, daughter, Dana, and son, David. They all reside in Dallas. David, by the way, is an SMU graduate and I am happy to say a brother Phi Delt!

My sister, Cynthia, was born on June 14, 1928, and married her high school sweetheart, Joe Johnson on July 14, 1949. Joe played quarterback in high school and at Occidental College, where he majored in Economics. He is a good guy, and fit into the family with ease. Like my dad, he was a member of the Alpha Tau Omega Fraternity. Their wedding reception was at the Country Club house, following their marriage at St. Mathews Episcopal Church in South Pasadena. My folks fixed up the apartment over the garage for them, while Joe finished up his senior year, graduating in 1950.

They have three children, Susan, Barbara and Robert. Joe worked in several fields, including a number of years with Hughes Aircraft Company. Cynthia died of breast Cancer in January 1967. She was 39. After a couple of tough years, Joe became a Flight Attendant for Northwest Airline and Delta, and after 26 years is still flying!

EARLY EXPERIENCES

In 1939 our family moved from Los Angeles to a suburb called Alhambra, where we had a California-style bungalow on Curtis Ave, corner of Hellman. I believe I had a normal upbringing for those times. We had a dog, Skipper, and a duck named Elmer... who was known for his pinch! There were plenty of kids in the neighborhood, and we played hide and seek and kick-the-can in the street. We came home when the street lights came on or my dad whistled. I also recall the whistle of the Helms Bakery man in his truck (always a highlight) and the toot of the fresh fish man as well. Yes, we had bottles of milk with cream on top delivered every week day.

I attended kindergarten and first grade at Marguerita Grammar School, which was only a few blocks away, but across the tracks of the Pacific Electric "red car" Streetcar. When my mom took me to the doctor, we took the red car to Los Angeles. What a shame that immediately after the war, the tracks were torn up and the cities went to buses powered by overhead electrical lines. What wonderful right of ways the red car tracks would have made for an urban mass transit system today!

I recall with great clarity the morning of Sunday, December 7, 1941. I was on the swing in the backyard when my dad came tearing out of the back porch shouting that the "Japanese had bombed Pearl Harbor!" Everyone in the neighborhood could hear him, and most thought he had "lost it," but he had been listening to the radio when it was first announced. I remember thinking, "Where is Pearl Harbor?" It was quite a vivid memory.

Shortly after Grandpa's retirement from the Los Angeles Water and Power Company, my mother's parents, Hattie and Samuel Billings, moved in with us. This was probably the reason we moved to a bigger house. I suppose it was the thing to do in those days, to make room for your folks. There were distinct pluses and minuses to that arrangement in my opinion. Grandma and Grandpa lived with us until their passing in the mid-1950s. Mom was anemic, and brought Ellen on to help look after the family two or three days a week.

MOVING TO SAN GABRIEL

In 1943, we leased a big bungalow in San Gabriel, at 623 Hermosa Dr. It was at least a couple of acres and came complete with a barn. It was a little further from Los Angeles, and had a more rural atmosphere than Alhambra. My brother, Lad, graduated from high school and joined the Navy. Dad and Grandpa developed quite a garden on the property, which was the thing to do in those days with the war and all. Actually, the entire country got into the war effort, not just those who served. We had corn, tomatoes, potatoes, beans, beets, squash and whatever else. I got my first lesson in weeding there. Gophers were quite a problem too. We still had Skipper, but Elmer didn't make the cut.

The family was in the house proper, with Ellen (who had joined us full-time) in a separate little guest house on the property. Her black retriever was named Bing (an African Setter she said) and her black Manx cat was named Anthracite, "Anty" for short. Ellen was with us, certainly with me at least, as long as I can remember with early photographs to confirm. While my mother, grandmother and Ellen all cooked, Ellen, who was from rural Georgia, introduced to the family what became known in the 1960's as "soul food." Remembering that Southern Blacks only got what wasn't used by the Whites, they did creative things with what they got. I was raised on black-eyed peas and ham hocks, corn bread, grits, fried liver, kidneys, tripe and brains, pickled pigs feet and boiled tongue. Loved it! Every race/culture has it's favorite and unique foods. Liking or disliking it is a function of when you are introduced to it.

ANOTHER MOVE!

Much too soon after we moved into the Hermosa property, 1944 or '45, the owner of the property "sold it out from under us" according to my dad. While he wasn't happy about it, there wasn't much he could do. We had to move again. We didn't go far. We bought a large (13 room, two story) home on an acre of land on Country Club Drive, just across from the 17th fairway of the private, San Gabriel Country Club. The house was built in 1910 by the old silent film star, Edward Everett Horton. It was in the process of being re-modeled when we bought it. For example, it had no electricity, it was all piped for gas lighting! It was not hooked up to a sewer, and needed lots of work in modernizing the kitchen and bathrooms. The master bath had a huge tub in it, a good 6 feet long, and sitting on four metal feet. Mom painted the feet gold and the outside of the tub pink with a big red rose on the side and a couple of pearls on the rose as dew drops!

There was plenty of room for all of us, a big apartment like space over the garage, and quarters for Ellen just off the kitchen. It was a great party house with lots of room for entertaining. The folks threw big parties for the oil crowd. I recall meeting with "Dutch" Lortcher, the President of Signal Oil and Gas and other luminaries.

Everyone smoked and most drank gin martinis or manhattans. I tried everything! I must say my mom was an outstanding hostess, and everyone loved her. She was not only a wonderful mother, but a huge asset in my dad's career!

CHURCH

Mom was raised a strong Episcopalian, while dad was a Presbyterian. Needless to say, his conversion to the Episcopal Church was a foregone conclusion! They were married at St. Mathias Episcopal Church in Los Angeles in 1924. My brother, sister, and I were all baptized and confirmed in the Episcopal Church. My dad, brother, and I all served on the vestries of our respective churches.

My first memory of going to church was in the early 1940's at the Holy Trinity Episcopal Church in Alhambra, following our move to San Gabriel. It was a small, old church. My brother and I were acolytes there (and actually served together on occasion). Dad was on the vestry and my grandmother, who did beautiful embroidery, embroidered all the priest's vestments. During the war, we transferred to the Church of our Savior in San Gabriel, which was much closer to us. That church is the oldest Episcopal Church on the West coast, and many have said the oldest protestant church as well, being founded in 1867. In addition to the old and lovely church (another larger one has since been built next to it), there is a cemetery there as well, where my grandparents are buried.

GENERAL GEORGE S. PATTON

The church has many beautiful stained glass windows, most of them having been given by a wealthy San Gabriel family, the Patton

Family. That is the family of General George S. Patton of World War II fame. When I was in Sunday school one Sunday during the war, General Patton came to speak to us in the small parish hall. All the youngsters were there. It was a long time ago, but I will never forget him walking into the hall. He was tall and straight and wearing a shiny helmet with three stars on it. There were stars on his shoulders, stars on his collar, campaign ribbons all over his chest, and two big pearl handled pistols at his sides. He wore beige jodhpurs tucked into shiny brown riding boots and carried a crop. We were awed beyond words. He stood up on the stage and took off his helmet, revealing his thin gray hair. He cleared his throat and told us about his experience as a boy at the church. Tears ran down his cheeks as he related how important religion and church are to us as Americans, and how fortunate we are that we have the freedom to choose where we worship in our wonderful country.

We were all spellbound, and I will never forget him standing there looking out at us through his tears. He was truly a man bigger than life. General Patton was in the U.S. on a war bond drive with General Jimmy Doolittle, of Tokyo bombing fame. My dad took me to the San Marino City Hall that afternoon to hear them both speak at a bond rally. Another special time.

While the war was still on, Grandpa went from the vegetable garden on the Hermosa property to chickens (Rhode Island Reds and Plymouth Rocks) and rabbits at the back of the country club property. We always had eggs, chicken, and rabbit to eat. Grandpa also skinned the rabbits and stretched their pelts on wire frames. When they were cured, he sold the pelts. He was fond of his local red wine, which he stashed in a little shed next to the rabbits. My buddies and I found the wine, gallon jugs, and would help ourselves to a taste every now and then.

My mom and I would go to the local horsemeat market to buy meat for the dogs… it was dyed blue so people would know it was horsemeat! Might be hard to believe today, but not in the 40s during wartime!

GROWING UP

When we moved from Alhambra to San Gabriel, I transferred to the Washington Grammar School and, for some reason, skipped 3rd grade. While my folks seemed pleased, it proved to be a persistent problem for me for several reasons. One was that I was immature, and also, short. Furthermore, I was now competing with kids a year older, both in sports as well as scholastics. I had poor study habits and loved to talk in class. As a result, I became an expert chalk eraser cleaner.

There was an active Cub Scout program, and I had lots of fun with my buddies in Den 10. We were competitive in sponsored sports programs with other dens. I worked my way up to the top, and received my "Weblos" badge.

When I graduated in 1948, I was the second shortest boy in our class at 5'3". Since I was a year younger, I was also the last to drive a car.

I grew 8" at Alhambra High School high school, but did not outgrow my poor study habits! I did win varsity letters in golf and track, as well as the affections of Joan Johnson. When we met she was a freshman and I was a sophomore. We dated and then went "steady" (most of the time). Her family lived about 5 minutes from us in San Gabriel. She was the only child of Marvin Goodwin Johnson and Mae Sanders Johnson. Joan was born in Dixon, Illinois on April 4, 1935.

Her parents were originally from Superior, Wisconsin (Norwegian and Swedish stock). Marvin wrestled and played a number of sports in high school. After college, he became a high school coach. They came West early in World War II. He opened a real estate office on Valley Boulevard in Rosemead, California (close to San Gabriel) and ran a successful business there for many years. Joan's mother was an only child, but Marvin had four brothers. Most of them came West as well, and settled in greater Los Angeles.

When I graduated from high school in 1952, I wanted to go to UCLA to stay close to Joan, while my dad pushed me to go to Cal. It was all moot in the end, as my grades were not good enough for either. So I began my college education at the Pasadena City College where I joined a local fraternity (Alpha Sigma Tau) and enjoyed my first year, socially at least, as reflected by my not-noteworthy grades.

Around this time, I bought my first car, a 1950 Ford business coupe for $250. It had been a Belridge Oil company car that dad arranged for me to purchase. It had spent all its time on private property up in the oil fields and so was in fine shape. Business coupes aren't made anymore, but they were mostly used for company cars or delivery. There was no back seat, just a rubber mat. No radio or air conditioning, stick shift, black wall tires and absolutely no chrome trim anywhere. It was, of course, black. It served me well through college, until I bought my brother's 1955 Fairlane Ford Tudor. A big step up!

UCLA MEMORIES

At some point I contacted the Admissions Office at UCLA for an interview and assessment of my transcripts. I met with a counselor who told me that I would be admitted "IF" I got a least a B average on all my required coursework for a year. This was my "Aha!"

moment. I did better than a B average, was elected Sophomore Class President, and was admitted to UCLA commencing in January, 1955. I joined the Phi Delta Theta Fraternity (Cal Gamma). This was truly a turning point in my life.

I have wonderful memories of my time at UCLA and the fraternity. I worked summers to make spending money, which was augmented by "hashing" on sorority row. "Hashing" means at noon you leave class, walk to the sorority house (Alpha Chi Omega), set up the lunch table, serve lunch, clear the table, eat your own meal, and wash the dishes. Then head for your next class. I did this for 2 years, hashing for lunch and dinner for meals and $5.00 a month. Fridays were beer bust time on fraternity row (often with the ladies) so more often than not, the hashers would show up for the evening meal at the sorority a little inebriated, appearing with cooking pots on our heads or worse. We were promptly fired by the House Mother, but usually re-hired the next week. Ah, college in the 50s!

Another fun memory of the fraternity at 535 Gayley Avenue in Westwood, was that our house was a two story with a big deck on the 2nd floor facing the street. One spring, someone came up with the idea of using balloons for water bags, and launching them from the deck onto unsuspecting pedestrians or passing cars. One fateful day, one of the brothers launched a balloon which went right into our mailman's delivery bag, and, he filed a complaint. A federal offense! I don't recall how long we were suspended from school activities by the university, but we escaped the federal charges. Probably because the FBI agent who came to the house was a former fraternity member and understood what great guys fraternity members really were!

The Phi Delts won the Spring Sing at the Hollywood Bowl in 1956 and also the Intramural Championship in sports. I scored in the 220 and 440 yard dashes and also pulled in the chariot race. My senior year I made the Dean's List in Economics. My high school teachers would never have believed it! I had enough credits for a degree in Political Science as well, but in those days you could only get one bachelor's degree at a time, so I took my degree in Economics.

I "pinned" Joan at a fraternity party in 1956, and my Best Man at the wedding was one of my pledge brothers, Tom Hinrichs. My brother Lad was an usher. Joan and I were married at Saint Edmunds Episcopal Church in San Marino, California, on February 9, 1957. The reception was at my folk's country club home, and it was a first-class affair! Several hundred people were there, and the house accommodated them easily. Joan and I left at some point for the Riverside Inn, and the next day, we left for Las Vegas and the Grand Canyon where we had a wonderful ten-day honeymoon. We returned to an apartment we had rented in San Gabriel, and set up house.

SPUTNIK I

I remember standing on the driveway in 1957 and looking up into the heavens. There it was, Russia's SPUTNIK I, a white dot gliding by the stars (in an elliptical low Earth orbit). I found it unsettling to say the least, as did many Americans, and a big wake-up call for the United States!

NAVY CRUISES

After graduating from high school in 1952, the Korean War (Conflict) was still going on, and I was drafted. I wanted to go on to college directly, so I joined the U.S. Naval Reserve for a four-year hitch, later extended to eight years. I attended drills every week at the armory in Pasadena and spent at least two weeks every summer on a "cruise," or navy school. My first year was "boot camp" at the San Diego Naval Training Center (USNTC) where we were taught basic marching and seamanship... as well as how to properly make up your bunk, stow your uniform in your locker, and wash your own skivvies, socks, dungarees and hats by hand. We'd hang them from the yardarm to dry in front of the barracks. Oh, you got a world class haircut too, and shots for every possible disease known to man! The shots were organized such that there were corpsmen on two sides of a passageway. "Boots," us new recruits, walked between them getting stabbed repeatedly by progressively duller needles until we were through. About one third of my company passed out in the process.

Boot Camp, San Diego Naval training Center, 1953

I was made company commander of roughly 80 boots. Selection was an arduous task. The Chief Petty Officer, who ran our lives, yelled "Who can count cadence?" With my scouting background I knew how to do that, and raised my hand among a number of others. The chief pointed at me and said "You're the company commander!" It was my first leadership position and I learned a great deal from the experience. During required summer duty, I attended schools such as Instructors School, and went on two major cruises. The first cruise in 1954 to Cuba, via the Panama Canal, and the second to the Far East in 1956.

My first ship was a Destroyer Escort (DE), the USS Weeden, DE 797. It was built during WW2 and commonly known as a "Tin Can," which was an apt description! This class of ship is nominally 300' long with a beam of 37' and carries a complement of 200 or so sailors and 10 officers. The mission of such ships was to protect slow moving convoys during the war. They were fast, reaching up to 24 knots. Very lightly armored and 'thin skinned" it would definitely not be my choice of ship in a shooting war. It had no air conditioning, meaning that the mess deck and sleeping compartments were always hot and smelly. When the 3" guns were fired, light bulbs in the ship burst and pipes leaked. Our primary mission was *patch, patch, patch*.

We had liberty in Acapulco, Mexico, and then steamed down to Panama. There were three DE's in our cruise, and all three ships were put in the same "lock" to go through the canal. This indicates the size of our ships and also the locks. As I recall, the first lock was named the "Mira Flores." We had liberty at the Rodman Naval Station (since closed), and could buy cans of cold beer for a nickel! We quickly learned that lots of beer coupled with hot, humid weather equaled bad headaches.

I have to relate the story of our ship's bosun mate. I don't remember his name, but I will never forget his tattoos. Like everything on a DE, shower facilities are small. Perhaps there were 10 shower heads. I was showering one morning when our bosun mate came in with his bathing gear. I noticed when his back was to me that he had a large "screw" or propeller tattooed on each cheek of his rear end. When he turned towards me, I saw he had "Sweet" and "Sour" tattooed on each pectoral. There were more tattoos on his stomach; a tattoo of a fox chasing a rabbit into his navel. Only the rear end of the rabbit disappearing into his navel was visible. I thought to myself, "Wow, now that is creative!" But wait, there was more. It took a lot of sideways peeking for me to figure out the rest of his tattoos, but I did. Ready? On his penis was a tattoo of a snake (multi-colored) wrapped around the length, with the snake's open mouth at the end.... fangs and all! Perched at the very tip was a small butterfly. OMG! I can't imagine. Now there is a real "salt" for you!

Once we cleared the Canal and headed for Havana, we tied up at the United Fruit Dock. We were there for three days, and enjoyed going ashore. I toured the old fort at the mouth of the harbor, the Monument to the Maine, and many other places. The president of Cuba in those days was General Fulgencio Batista, and at night, the place to go was called the Tropicana. It was a full scale night club with large glass or plastic tubes hanging from the ceiling that animals like panthers or tigers would walk through. Very impressive! Drinking Cuba Libres (rum and coke) was the thing, and we consumed many of them! Our liberty was usually up at midnight, but the captain was at the club one night, along with most of the crew, (probably as well-oiled as we were), and extended liberty for all hands until 2:00 a.m. Just what we needed!

My second cruise was very different. The Navy organized a cruise called "Operation Deployment West" in 1956. Only a few reservists could go. I put in for it, and was selected. We flew commercially from San Diego to San Francisco, and then were bussed to the U.S. Naval Air Station at Moffett Field. We boarded a Navy DC-6, and flew to Midway Island, and then Kwajalein Island for fuel, finally landing at the U.S. Naval Air Station, Atsugi, Japan, on the island of Kyushu. We were then bussed to our ship, the USS Roanoke, CL 145, (a light cruiser) which was berthed at our naval base in Sasebo.

USS ROANOKE

She was a beautiful ship, 679' long with a 70' beam and cruised at 33 knots. She had white oak decks and, thankfully, air conditioning. On a cruiser, more formal uniforms were required. Whereas enlisted men wore dungarees and a chambray shirt on the DE, the cruiser required us to don our whites. The crew complement was 1400 officers and enlisted. Our Captain, E.T. Sands, had not been selected for rear admiral, and so was unhappily heading for retirement. The bridge became a rather depressing place to be when he was present.

We departed Sasebo, and set sail for Nagasaki, Japan. This was the city that had the second atomic bomb dropped on it. While much of the rubble had been cleaned up, there were many stark reminders of the immensity and effect of the blast. I will never forget touring the museum established to record the devastating effects of the bomb. I don't recall any contact with civilians that weren't very polite and accommodating.

We sailed from Nagasaki and headed south for Hong Kong Island. On our way, we did live firing of the twelve 6" guns, six forward in two turrets and six aft in two turrets. On the bridge, where I was, we removed the glass windows so they wouldn't be damaged by the blasts. We were about 50 feet from the guns, and when they fired (three barrels at a time) there was an incredible concussive wave that pressed in on you and especially your ears. We had no ear protection, and while all this was going on it was impossible to keep your hands over your ears (for what good that did) and still do your job. When the 6" guns weren't firing, the twelve 3" 50s along the sides of the ship were, along with twenty-four 20mm guns. Fourth of July with a really big bang!

We arrived in Hong Kong, and anchored "in the stream" between the island and the mainland. It was the prime spot, which we were granted due to our captain's seniority. We enjoyed striking views of Victoria Peak and the impressive harbor.

No sooner had we anchored, when the captain's barge was lowered and headed towards shore, empty. In the meantime, the ship was surrounded by dozens of small "bum boats" holding 2 or 3 persons equipped with long poles. It appeared that the Navy had cut a deal with the locals (remember that this was in the mid-50s). The deal was the "Hong Kongese" would paint the hull with Navy paint using rollers mounted on long poles. In return, they would get the ship's garbage. After chow, you would take your tray to the line of garbage cans and scrape off what was left, receiving a big toothy smile from the Chinese person collecting the left-overs…. and there were a lot! An early "food for work" program!

THE CAPTAIN'S GUEST

In the midst of all this, the captain's barge returned from shore with one passenger. A beautiful young Chinese woman came aboard.

She wore a traditional silk dress with a high collar, with slits on both sides well up the thigh. Believe me, none of the crew missed it! She was taken immediately to the captain's quarters, and wasn't seen again until she departed three days later, just before we hoisted anchor to depart. Good for Captain Sands, navigating his way to retirement through the arms of a lovely lady!

We had the opportunity to do a lot of sight-seeing—taking in the view from Victoria Peak of Kowloon and the harbor, Repulse Bay, floating restaurants, Tiger Balm Gardens and little shops selling all sort of exotic things. I bought and was fitted for a herringbone, double vent sport coat at one of the many tailor shops, and picked it up the next day. It was fully lined with my name sewn in. It fit me like a glove... and was cheap! One day, a buddy and I went to the Peninsula Hotel on the Kowloon side to look around and have a beer. At that time, it was owned by the British. It was the best hotel in Hong Kong, situated right on the water with a good view of our ship. We were in dress whites, and went up the steps to the front doors, only to be intercepted by the doorman who advised that sailors were not welcome. I wanted to tell him that we had been refused entry into better places than the Peninsula Hotel, but I couldn't think of one.

The price of property in Hong Kong is unbelievably high. The Chinese, being very creative, have made the island bigger and built huge high rises where there was once only water. The Peninsula Hotel, which was on the water in the 1950s, is now a block from the water, and its scenic view is blocked by the new Space Museum! It won't be long, at the present pace, until you will be able to walk from the island to the mainland!

LINUS DETZER

Our next stop was the Philippine Islands and our port, Manila, was the Navy base at Subic Bay. It was hot and humid. For liberty, if you were in the "mood for love," you went to the town of Olangapo, a classic port town. My parents had an old friend in the islands, Linus Detzer, and arranged for me to visit him. When I got ashore, he was waiting in a chauffeured limousine! "Detz" knew my folks from high school so they went way back. He was the U.S. Steel Company representative in the Philippines and was there when the Japanese invaded. He took me to his apartment, which was right on Dewey Boulevard, running along the bay. The tallest building along the Bayfront, there were 4 or 5 floors and Detz's apartment took up the whole top floor. There was a lovely covered porch with wonderful views of the bay, which still teemed with rusting ship hulls. As a bachelor, he had two Philippine ladies in his life: a house-keeper and a cook. These ladies insisted on washing my uniform. They put me in a nice robe, handed me a cold San Miguel Beer, and seated me on the porch for a talk with Detz. Yesss!

He told me that when the Japanese came, they did not enter his building for several days. He recalled that the soldiers tried to start various cars in the street, but didn't understand the requirement for an ignition key so, they pressed on the starter button until each car battery was dead. One apparently threw a hand grenade in the elevator shaft, putting it out of commission. Someone eventually told the Japanese about him and they took him into custody. He was in the Bataan Death March, and his stories were terrifying. He was imprisoned at the Santo Tomas Camp for the duration. Detz said the only thing that kept him alive was his faithful housekeeper who slipped him food through the fence. He lost all his teeth, but regained his weight and general health and returned to the U.S. to retire. As for me, the ship returned to Sasebo, Japan, and we flew home. The cruise was a superb experience.

A HELPING HAND

I would hope that everyone has experiences in life where some-one reached out and extended a helping hand. During my years at UCLA, I attended naval reserve meetings in Santa Monica. During the summer I also worked for the Macco Company out East in Covina. The drive to attend the weekly reserve meetings in Santa Monica was a killer, taking 2 to 3 hours each way and I had to be at the Macco Yard to catch my truck to the worksite by 6:30 in the morning. Ugly!

The commanding officer of our reserve unit was Lt. Commander Bill Simmons, and he knew I was attending UCLA, spending my summer at home in San Gabriel. He was kind enough to offer to sponsor me for Officer Candidate School (OCS), which I declined because I wanted to get married after graduation, and OCS had a 3-year active Navy commitment with it. What he was able to do for me during the summers was above and beyond. He said if I called him on the day of each reserve meeting and told him "I was alive," he would cover for me. This saved me that awful trip every week! You never forget that kind of help.

In 1958, Joan's dad gave us a 50' x 100' lot in Rosemead, California, just south of San Gabriel. We put the lot up as collateral, and ob-tained a construction loan. We built a 1000 sq. ft. (2 bedrooms, one bath) home for a total payment of $25.00 a month. That was just what we needed when starting out at North American Aviation's Autonetics Division. Our first son, Howard, was born two years later on October 14, 1959, at Saint Luke's in Pasadena. I finished my eight-year obligation in 1961, and was honorably discharged from the naval reserve, and our second son Paul was born on June 30, 1962 at the Methodist Hospital in Arcadia, California. Our family lived in Rosemead until we moved to the Yorba Linda/Placentia area in Orange County in 1965 to be close to work.

There we bought a new 3 bedroom/2 bath home at 5111 McKenzie Drive for $27,500. My dad had a fit, but that was what it cost in those days. It was in a good neighborhood and school district and everything worked out fine. Yorba Linda was also the birthplace of Richard Nixon; Joan and President Nixon's mother, Hanna, were friends.

Autonetics built quite a complex in Anaheim on Mira Loma Avenue, including half a dozen large, single story buildings, and a five story headquarters building. It was a beautiful campus, lots of grass, trees and parking. From our new home to work was an easy 10-minute drive. With a company like Autonetics in the neighborhood, it didn't take long for a "watering hole" to appear across the street from the headquarters building on Mira Loma Avenue. I don't remember the name, but it quickly became a favorite spot for after work drinks and conversation. I learned many things from sitting with the top two engineers on the Mark II Program: Bob Greer, Chief Engineer, and Norm Hesgard, Chief of Avionics.

CHAPTER TWO

Early Work Experience: To 1968

When I was old enough to get a job, we lived in San Gabriel. My first "real" job was a paper route for the Los Angeles Times Mirror. In high school, I worked as a salesman at Woodruffs Men's Store in Alhambra. For three years or so during Christmas break I sold shirts, ties, sweaters and accessories, making $1.00/hour until my last year, when I asked for, and received a $.25 raise! Lesson learned. In the early 1950s I worked for two gas stations during summer vacations-- Coburn and Hyatt's Union Oil station in San Gabriel, and a Chevron station near the Santa Anita Race Track in Arcadia.

The Union station had an old rotary Coke machine. It's interesting how you remember certain things...You put in your nickel, turned the crank, lifted the lid and removed the cold bottle. Life was good! The Union gas station was a "full service" station. We checked a customer's oil, battery, radiator levels, and tire pressure. Then we used a whiskbroom to clean the floor in the front of the car, and, of course, the windshield. For those efforts, I made $1.05 to $1.25per hour. Gas was about $0.25 a gallon. In my day, they were "service stations." Today they are "gas stations" with no service.

In college, I worked Christmas vacations at the San Gabriel Post Office delivering parcel post. I don't remember how much I made, but I drove a Ford station wagon (like we all did), and if we saw one another during our deliveries, we drag raced. One of the regular mail men witnessed one of these races and reported it to the Postmaster... luckily no one was identified! The best part of the job was that my family's home on Country Club Dr., as well as my girlfriend's house on Willard Ave., were on my route! Both places offered a ready refuge, plus a glass of milk and a cookie to ease me through my long and hectic work schedule!

EARTH SCULPTING

My last two years of summer jobs were with the MACCO Pipeline Company (MacCloud Construction). The company installed natural gas mains and service lines to houses in new tracts in the Covina area. The first year I was mostly a laborer, spending long days on the business end of a shovel. But I also had numerous opportunities to be the "PTO" man, that is the pneumatic tool operator, operating a clay spade or jackhammer. I made $1.25/hour with the shovel, but when I was the PTO man, I made $1.75/hour. Being a union job, if I was PTO man for 4 hours or more during a shift, I was paid for the entire shift as PTO man. Big bucks indeed!

I learned important lessons from digging gas service lines. The soil we worked was sandy and gravelly. Digging a 3-foot-deep trench was made even more difficult because the sides would give way and collapse into the trench. So, while the trench was 3 feet deep, it was also 4 to 5 feet wide. Have I mentioned it was really hot? The lesson here is that you do not want to make this your life's work!

One day I put down my shovel and walked over to our truck for a drink of water. On my way, I passed one of my co-workers, a heavy, short man in his late 40s named, Gilberto, who was busy digging his trench. I could not help but notice that, while not perfect, his trench was much narrower than mine. I was impressed, and told him so. I asked him what his secret was. He said something like "my friend, in life you will always find that every person you meet can do at least one thing better than you can." From that encounter I learned to look at the people you meet (regardless of status) with the thought in mind that they can do at least one thing better than you can. Acknowledging this engenders a receptive attitude from the person you are addressing. When you start every interaction by demonstrating respect, an open, honest, dialogue becomes much more likely. I also believe it adds a measure of dignity that might otherwise be absent. The flip side is also true: no matter the perceived talents of someone you meet, there is likely at least one thing you can do better than them. Another life lesson.

DEEP DITCH WORK

My second summer with MACCO was spent in Glendale, California. The company was installing a major new gas supply line in the city. I worked as a roustabout, doing everything from installing shoring in the 20-foot-deep trench to directing the 30" pipe, which was held in a sling by a side-boom caterpillar tractor. As the tractor moved slowly forward, I stood on the front end of the pipe and guided it down through the shoring to the bottom of the trench. There were some exciting times!

I was making $1.90/hour. To avoid paying a penalty, the company had to guarantee the city of Glendale that the street would not be closed to traffic longer than three days per block. However, when you are working at 20 foot depths, cave-ins are sure to happen. And they did! To avoid the penalty, the company paid us overtime and usually Saturday work, all at time and one-half. Fortunately, I was living with my folks, so I could save money. After two years of summer work, I had enough money to buy my future wife, Joan Johnson, a diamond engagement ring... paid in full with cash.

In 1957, after graduating from UCLA, I went to work for the Southwestern Engineering Company in Vernon, California. This was a good interim job while I completed some company interviews and focused on what I wanted to do with my life. Southwestern primarily manufactured heat exchangers and pressure vessels for the process and petro-chemical industries. I was in production control under a nice fellow named Wayne Warner. He helped me appreciate work flow, the shop floor, and the manufacturing process. A very useful experience early in my career.

In the meantime, I interviewed with the Dow Chemical Company and IBM. Both companies wanted me to join them and attend their training schools, in Michigan and New York respectively. However, I heeded my dad's advice which was to join a company that had its headquarters in a place where you ultimately wanted to live because you would be successful and end up in the corporate office... dad was always a positive thinker! Another lesson here.

NORTH AMERICAN AVIATION & AUTONETICS

In 1958, I interviewed with the Autonetics Division of North American Aviation. The division was the corporation's electronics capability. Other divisions manufactured fighter and bomber aircraft such as, the P-51, F-86, F-100, XB-70 and the B-1. The Rocketdyne Division manufactured liquid-fueled rocket engines for manned space flight. Though IBM offered the most money at $500.00 a month, Autonetics offered $420.00 a month, and I would get to stay in Southern California! Corporate Headquarters were on Imperial Highway, close to the Los Angeles Airport (see, dad, I listened to you!). North American Aviation was a NYSE listed company and I spent 10 rewarding years there.

Autonetics was located on the campus of the old World War II Vultee Aircraft Plant at the corner of Lakewood Blvd. and Imperial Hwy. in Downey, California. The corporation's Navigation Systems Division, which had the prime contract on the Apollo Program, was also located there. We all enjoyed the huge open hangar areas, asphalt floors, and electrical plugs hanging down from the ceiling!

Autonetics designed and manufactured airborne computers, radar systems, fire and flight control systems, and automatic checkout equipment. Among other things, we designed and built the computer for the GAM-77 missile carried by B-52's and had the guidance contract for the MINUTEMAN ICBM.

The late 50s were a watershed time in the aerospace world. Technology was shifting from analog to digital. While I had no problem with it, many senior engineers who cherished their slide rules, resisted the change from vacuum tubes to solid state devices. Resistance, of course, was futile. Yet another life lesson.

I went to work in the Computer and Data Systems Division on the staff of the Chief Engineer, Dr. Norman Parker. After a year or so, I wanted to work in an engineering project office and be involved in programs. I transferred into an office where I learned a lot of useful technical and operational information from Ken Giles and his staff. One of the really neat things we were involved in was the flight control system for the X-15 aircraft.

THE X-15

The X-15 was a hypersonic research aircraft, and was designed to be carried aloft and drop-launched under the wing of a NASA B-52 mother ship. Scott Crossfield, a company pilot, was the first to fly the aircraft in June 1959. This was also my first connection with Neil Armstrong. Though best known as being the first man to set foot on the moon, Armstrong made a number of flights in the X-15 as well.

The X-15 holds the official world record for the highest speed ever recorded by a manned, rocket-powered aircraft, reaching up to 4,520 mph (Mach 6.72). The X-15 is on exhibit at the Smithsonian Air and Space Museum in Washington, D.C. and I strongly encourage everyone to visit the many historic aircraft and space vehicles on display there.

Periodically, we would take a company Aero Commander aircraft to Edwards Air Force Base to update the X-15's flight control system. I was so impressed by how small it was, especially the cockpit. It was a real thrill to be there.

On one trip, we landed and taxied toward the X-15 hanger. Suddenly, the pilot shut off an engine, faking a problem, and stopped the aircraft. "Look at that!", he yelled, pointing out the starboard side. I looked where he was pointing and saw a squat, sharp edged, nasty looking aircraft. With its nose pointed at us, it was parked in a dirt revetment. We later learned this was the first SR-71 at

Edwards for secret flight tests of a brand new, very advanced reconnaissance (spy) aircraft.

Suddenly, a jeep pulled up alongside our plane, and MP's were pointing weapons at us, telling the pilot to get "that piece of shit moving!" He did. I will never forget what an impressive thing it was. I don't know if there will ever be a more elegant or more capable aircraft than the SR-71. It was then and remains now the fastest manned, jet-powered aircraft in existence. It reached speeds of 2,193.13 mph, and could cruise at 80,000 feet.

CONTRACTS & PRICING DEPARTMENT

After spending three years in engineering, I had learned the basics: how subsystems tie together in a system (the sum of its parts are greater than the whole), how it all relates to an aircraft and its mission, and many other relevant things. Ready to make a change, I joined the Contracts and Pricing Department and went to work in the new business proposal group. The 1960's were ripe with new business opportunities fostered by rapidly advancing technologies, software, and international problems. I headed up major efforts on the MMRBM (Mobile Medium Range Ballistic Missile) Proposal, and a classified 477L program named Nuclear Detection System (NUDETS).

FIRST BUSINESS TRIP

I was also assigned an existing contract for a recorder/reproducer for the F-4 Phantom aircraft, called NADAR 8 (North American Digital Automatic Recorder, eight channel). It would record everything during a flight/mission, and then it could be re-played on the ground. The contract was with the Navy and was the reason for my first business trip to Washington, D.C. Autonetics offices were part of the corporate office in Washington, which were located in the Moreschi Building at 16th and K Streets, NW. Each division had its own representatives or marketing guys. I was introduced to Jim Taglia, who would join me in my meeting with the Navy. We had an OK meeting with the navy customer, who wasn't very keen on a program that "ratted out" what a pilot did wrong by replaying the recording after the fact. Anyway, Jim knew this was my first trip to Washington. At the end of the day he asked if I would like to go to the Gaslight Club on 17th Street for a drink at a time when "key clubs" were a big deal. I was delighted!

The club was at least three to four stories, and each floor had music, dancing, cocktails, and lovely ladies dressed in scant gay 90's garb… lots of legs and cleavage! I had a fine time, and never forgot Jim's looking after me. Unfortunately, sometime after this trip Jim carelessly left a "confidential" document in a taxi, losing his security clearance and his job. Another life lesson.

MANNED SPACE CRAFT

Another program that I was involved in was the DYNA-SOAR Program in which we bid on and won the central computer contract. Boeing won a contract in 1959 to build the manned space glider which would be powered by the TITAN III launch vehicle from Cape Canaveral, Florida. In November 1959, it was designated as the X-20, and in March 1962, 6 test pilots were assigned to the program. One of whom was Neil Armstrong, my second connection with him!

Autonetics was of course interested in the flight control system, based on its experience with the X-15. Our computer utilized a rotating ceramic disc memory with input/output via Clevite read/write heads. Our customer was a division of the Honeywell Corporation, based in St. Petersburg, Florida. The buyer I dealt with was Jack Bonner, a tough old timer. The lead engineer was a bright young man named Al Thalheimer. All our testing went well, until we ran into serious sinusoidal vibration problems. This occurred when there was engine ignition and thousands of pounds of engine thrust hit the ground and bounced back up into the flight vehicle. The extremely high vibration levels caused the computer's ceramic disc memory (which is separated from the Clevite heads by miniscule space), to scrape against the heads. We worked and worked on the problem but found no solution.

Before the computer became an issue, however, the U.S. Government cancelled the program. A major reason was its centrality to the political fight between the Air Force and NASA regarding which should have the responsibility for our manned space program. Unlike the NASA programs, Dyna-Soar allowed for controlled re-entry (actually landing the vehicle on the ground like the Space Shuttle as opposed to a parachute). This was where the main effort in the X-20 was placed. Then Secretary of Defense, Robert McNamara, directed the Air Force to undertake a study to determine which program was a more feasible approach to a space-based weapon system: NASA's GEMINI Program or the Air Force Dyna-Soar Program. After reviewing the study, McNamara stated "that the Air Force had placed too much emphasis on controlled re-entry when it did not have any real objectives for orbital flight." This was seen as a reversal of his earlier position. There was also some talk of the high cost of Dyna-Soar and the fact that it could not launch a manned mission until the mid-1960s, at the earliest.

This became an early and telling fight for the direction of America's manned space flight program.

APPALACHIA

Appalachia in the United States is not a well-defined cultural region. West Virginia, however, is widely considered at its center. While endowed with abundant natural resources, Appalachian culture has struggled and is often associated with poverty.

By the 1960s, the region, and West Virginia in particular, had failed to capitalize on its major industries: logging and coal mining. Presidential candidate John F. Kennedy campaigned in West Virginia, winning an early and important primary there. When he was President, he enacted a number of policies specifically geared toward relieving the poverty that had plagued West Virginia since the inception of statehood. These policies included highway construction and worker training programs, among many others.

Companies were always looking to score political "points," and when low labor costs were associated with them, distinct possibilities appeared. Through its Autonetics Division, North American Aviation decided to take advantage of the government's encouraging initiatives and invested in West Virginia. This could well have included financial incentives as well, but I was in no position to know.

They decided to establish a division outside of Bluefield, West Virginia. The plant would manufacture and assemble electrical cables and harnesses, among other things, to support various North American Division needs. I was asked to look at setting up the contracts and pricing function there. Ostensibly, if I wanted the job,

I would be the supervisor. From Los Angeles, I made a couple of transfers and arrived at Bluefield in a Convair-240, a twin engine piston commuter aircraft, probably Allegheny Airlines. I rented a car and drove to the plant site in a little town called Princeton.

I checked into the one-story hotel in town, where a nice lady showed me to my room. While looking around I noticed a tall glass of water on a table by the bed.

"That's a nice touch!" I commented.

She said, "You know, that's not water, it's White Lightening."

I must have looked puzzled because she went on to say, "You know, Moonshine."

"Oh!" I exclaimed, "That's even better!"

She took me over to the window and pointed out a house about one hundred feet from the hotel. "That's Mazie's house, where you'll have your breakfast tomorrow. Just follow the path." Let me tell you, I had the biggest breakfast of my life at Mazie's the next morning! It was incredible. She served up eggs any way you wanted them, thick smoked bacon, homemade biscuits and gravy, grits, blueberry pancakes with homemade jam, juice, and coffee. I gave her a big tip and the bill was still under $2!

I drove to the plant and met the general manager, his small staff, and about 30 employees. It looked well set up to me. Machines were running, long tables had been set up to bundle the harnesses, and everyone was busy working.

At the end of the day, I drove back into town and decided to look around a little. Everyone I ran into was very outgoing and friend-ly. Big smiles were in abundance! I stopped by the local hardware store, and went into the local bank. It was a classic old fashioned bank with tellers in a cage and all. On my way out, I noticed a big vase on the floor holding umbrellas. An employee told me that when it rained, customers were free to take one and bring it back on their next visit. Not happening in L.A.!

When I reported back to the office, I said the plant and employees were impressive. However, I was not interested in a supervisor position. Thanks for thinking of me! While I would have loved to be a supervisor, Princeton, West Virginia just wasn't the place for me or my family. As fate would have it, this turned out to be a good decision!

There was an extremely short period between President Kennedy's assassination in November 1963, and the closure of the plant in Princeton. Without the President, the entire policy of encouraging industrial development in West Virginia came to an abrupt end. I felt badly about the people affected. Politics!

DEPARTMENT OF DEFENSE POLICY DIRECTIVE

President Kennedy brought Robert McNamara from the Ford Motor Company to the Pentagon in January 1961. As Secretary of Defense, he wrought many changes, but none so pervasive or far reaching as Department of Defense Directive 3200.9. It was instituted in February, 1964 and entitled "Project Definition Phase" (PDP). In the past, potential weapon systems suffered from high costs and long development cycles. Part of the problem was that subsystems such as radars, inertial measurement units, and flight computers were purchased individually, and then tied together through software into a system. Innumerable changes fed into the system adding more complexity, delays, and higher costs.

The new directive was primarily oriented toward a methodical, competitive planning and definition—step function approach to a given development prior to a major commitment of national resources involved in final design, development, production, and deployment. The intent of PDP was to avoid an early commitment of resources to high risk developments, which often showed illusory promise of satisfying ill-defined requirements based on comparatively shallow studies of the basic requirements. In many cases, this placed too much reliance on over-optimistic contractors in highly competitive situations. Consequences were schedule slips, cost overruns, and frequently degraded physical and performance characteristics in the system. In many cases, these resulted in program cancellation and the loss of time and resources.

PDP was supposed to change all of that! In early 1965, it was superseded by an improved directive (bearing the same number) and entitled "Initiation of Engineering and Operational Systems Development." Defense companies were now looking at a different (and much more specific) set of requirements to compete and win systems-level contracts.

A NEW DIVISION

In order to be successful in this new environment, Autonetics decided to form a new division. In 1965 they created the Strike Avionics[1] Systems Division, which was dedicated to winning systems contracts. It would be located in Anaheim, California, about

---

1   Avionics are aviation electronics

45 minutes or so from the old Downey plant. The key point here is that instead of bidding on just a radar or flight computer, we would bid on an "integrated" system of all cockpit avionics, and it would be digital.

I very much wanted to be part of the new division, and landed a position in the new Contacts and Pricing organization as a Major Systems Proposal Coordinator. I would be responsible, along with the Proposal Manager, for ensuring that the technical, cost, and management proposals were completed on time and responsive to all the requirements of the government's Request for Proposal (RFP). Given the huge size and complexity of the proposals required, it was a big job, and one I relished.

INTEGRATED DIGITAL AVIONIC SYSTEMS

The first Government systems RFP out of the box under the new directive was called IHAS. It was for an Integrated Helicopter Avionics System for a new Army helicopter. We lost the competition to the Teledyne Systems Company, but it was a useful experience nonetheless. The next system RFP was for a Navy program, the Integrated Light Attack Avionics System (ILAAS) for the A-7 Aircraft. We went through the whole effort and submitted our first integrated systems proposal under the new government guidelines... which was an accomplishment! I don't remember which company won the contract, but I do know that it was cancelled early in the development process. The Government and Industry were having multiple problems under the new directive.

Next up was the Air Force. In 1965, it put out an RFP for an integrated avionics system for the F-111 aircraft, the Mark II. We worked hard for several months to get it all together. The men and women in the division were the best the company had and they left nothing to chance. Some weeks after we submitted our proposal, the Air Force called and invited a team to Wright Patterson Air Force Base in Dayton, Ohio where the Systems Program Office for the Mark II was located. Three of us went to enter negotiations: Tom McNary, (Mark II Program Director), Jake Brown, (Mark II Chief Engineer), and me as the Chief Negotiator. We learned early on that our competitors had been whittled down by the Air Force to General Dynamics and IBM. Worthy foes indeed!

Sometime during our presentation, Tom McNary got sideways with the Air Force negotiator, Bill Bidstrup. I don't know what he said or did, but we were told the meeting was over and that we were to leave! What a shock! However, a few days after our return to Anaheim the Air Force called and invited us back. This time, only Jake and I went. Tom McNary had been removed from the program. Our meeting went well with the Air Force and we returned home hopeful.

A week later, the Air Force called again inviting us to come back to Dayton for additional negotiations on our proposal. Technically we were up to snuff, so this time the company sent me by myself. I met our Dayton Office Vice President, John "Fitz" Fitzpatrick, and we went to the meeting at the Air Force Base. Mr. Bidstrup made clear early on that this was a very competitive situation, and that we should reconsider our price. I argued that our price was fair and reasonable and that we would stand by it. Fitz was twitching. To alleviate the tension, Mr. Bidstrup called for a 10-minute break. After we reconvened he said the Air Force would accept a maximum offer of $2.5 million, which was slightly less than our number. I asked for another short break and Fitz and I went into the hallway. Fitz was very excited and clamoring to accept the Air Force number (typical marketing guy!). I said I was going to accept, but I didn't want Mr. Bidstrup to think his offer was a slam dunk. We went back to the meeting and I accepted their offer, with slightly damp shorts! This initial contract grew to over a billion dollars, one of the first of its size and scope in the industry, establishing Autonetics as a major systems house.

A HUGE WIN!

Back at our Dayton Office we were ecstatic and phoned the good news to the general manager at the Strike Division in Anaheim, Leo Killen. We were officially in the Systems business! I returned home to a wonderful reception. My reward for the win was being named Manager of the Operations and Administration Department, a line job in the new division. I was 30 years old. What a thrill!

It is important to note that this was the first contract issued for an integrated digital avionics system for a tactical aircraft under the new DoD directive. For the first time, key subsystems such as fire control, flight computer, flight control, and inertial measurement unit would be able to communicate with each other utilizing the dual digital data buss in the MK II System. All military aircraft and commercial airliners today utilize this technology.

In the ensuing two years, we worked hard on the MK II development under the many requirements of the DoD directive. I enjoyed my job, and brought excellent staff into the department. We had about 20 talented and motivated people.

Department Manager, Autonetics, 1968

MAKING A DIFFENCE

With any new government procurement change, especially a major one like this, there are those that argue the pros and cons. I was deeply involved in our proposal effort, and working to meet all the new requirements that had been imposed on us in executing the program. As one of the first to work under the new "Engineering and Systems Development" directive, I encountered a number of things during both the proposal process and during the program that could be improved or were just missing. I wrote several articles about the problems I encountered. The first, "A Survey of Problems in System Development" was published in the *National Contract Management Journal* in the Spring of 1967. Another was published in the *Armed Forces Journal*, "Weapon System Management: Has the Potential Been Realized?" in May 1967, and the third, a 19-page article entitled "Major DoD Procurements at War with Reality" appeared in *The Harvard Business Review*'s January-February 1970 issue.

In the meantime, more attention within the industry was being paid to the importance and impact of Department of Defense Directive 3200.9. The Aerospace Industries Association in Washington, D.C. formed a working group to look into the effects of the directive on its member companies. Bernie Haber, one of our corporate vice presidents was on that working group and enlisted me to work with him and the committee in Washington.

Jim Grodsky, from the Department of Defense Research and Engineering offices (DDR&E) who had the DoD in-house responsibility for overseeing the directive, also called and invited me to come and discuss it with him at the Pentagon. We had many pertinent conversations and became friends in the process. Others such as U.S. Army General Rowney wanted me to address his staff, and NASA Headquarters invited me to speak to its people in Houston, Texas. This was all very flattering, but what was really exciting was the invitation from the Armed Forces Institute of Technology at Wright Patterson Air Force Base to address their class of senior grade officers from all branches of the military. Quite a heady wine for a 30-year-old aerospace manager from California!

Speaking at the Armed Forces Institute of Technology, Dayton, Ohio.
This was where I first learned of the White House Fellows Program

I went to the Air Force Institute and addressed the class. Following that, there were questions and spirited discussion regarding my thoughts on Systems Development. After it was all over, a Navy captain came up to me and asked if I had ever heard of the White House Fellows Program? I said I had not, and he pulled out his card, wrote a phone number on the back, and handed it to me. I put it in my pocket and thanked him. When I got back to my office in Anaheim and emptied everything out of my pockets, I found the card. I noticed that the captain had written a 202 area code number on it, which was Washington, D.C., a different number than the one on his card. Out of curiosity, I called the number and almost dropped the phone when it was answered, "White House, how may I help you?" I considered hanging up, but managed to mumble something about the White House Fellows… Nonplussed, the operator said, "Oh, fine, let me connect you."

CHAPTER THREE

The White House Fellows-
Johnson Administration: 1968

The White House Fellows Commission Office took my call. I said I was interested in the program, and we chatted briefly about some basic requirements: being 23-33 years old and not being a felon, among others. She said she would send me the application package.

So, what is the White House Fellows Program? In the late 1950s, philanthropist and Secretary of Health, Education and Welfare (to be), John Gardner, envisioned a program that would expose America's young men and women of "intelligence, character, special talents and general promise" to the nation's government. The goal was to create a "reservoir of men and women with more than ordinary comprehension of government and more than ordinary willingness to serve."

Gardner discussed this at length with President Johnson in 1964. Following their discussions, the President issued Executive Order 11183, creating the White House Fellowships. He also announced the appointment of a Presidential Commission to oversee the

Fellowships. Within days over 8,000 young men and women expressed interest in the program. The commission said, "More must be done in the development of our ablest young people to inspire and facilitate the emergence of such leaders and statesmen. Their horizons and experience must be broadened to give them a sense of personal involvement in the leadership of society, a vision of greatness for the society, and a sense of responsibility for bringing that greatness to reality."

The program design was straightforward. Fellows were assigned to Senior White House officials and Cabinet members as special assistants. Through their work they would participate in decision making at the highest levels and learn the lessons of leadership. This work was to be augmented by policy trips and off-the-record conversations "with leaders in government, military, diplomatic corps, press, business, labor, academia, science, philanthropy, and the arts."

The program is now in its 52nd year, having built a legacy of leadership and service to our nation. Being chosen from thousands of applicants changed my life.

I regret now that I didn't keep a copy of my application, but it wasn't so easy to do back then! It contained a number sections, including several essays, 500 words or less, on why you wanted to be a Fellow, and what you would bring to the program. It also asked for your community involvement, leadership positions in your profession, academic honors, publications, goals in life, and more. The application package detailed the educational backgrounds of the first three classes of Fellows (1964 to 1967). About one quarter held Ph.D. Degree's while the rest held Masters and/or law degrees. With a mere bachelor's degree, I was intimidated. But my competitive juices were up, and I finished the application and sent it off. "Nothing ventured, nothing gained." A life lesson.

BECOMING A FELLOW

Perhaps a month later, I received a letter with additional difficult questions. I did my best to answer. Several weeks passed and then I received a third letter advising me that I had been selected as a "Regional Finalist" (there were 12 regions in the country) and should report to the Civil Service Commission Office in San Francisco. They advised I should be prepared to stay for several days of interviews and meetings with a panel of "notables" from the San Francisco area. The chairman was Dean Arbuckle of the Stanford Business School. On the afternoon we arrived, we gathered in a large auditorium. Looking at the men and women assembled, there had to have been 150 regional finalists. A lot, I thought!

Dean Arbuckle opened the meeting, explaining that we would start that afternoon with an open debate, followed by cocktails and dinner. The next two days would follow suit; we would be interviewed by pairs of regional panel members, with cocktails and dinner following each evening. I don't clearly remember much of these meetings and interviews. Everything was a blur of activity. But I do recall that after the panel had been introduced, Dean Arbuckle asked the following question: "Do you believe the United States should mine the Straits of Malacca, cutting off supplies to North Vietnam?"

A deafening silence followed. Remember, this was 1968, and the Vietnam War was in full bloom. I thought well, this is not the time to be bashful. If the whole idea was to generate debate, I needed to stand up and say something. I raised a solitary hand and was quickly called upon. I stood up and gave an off the cuff rationale that the U.S. should mine the Straits. When I finished, the auditorium erupted in a sea of hands and shouts…the battle had commenced!

Several weeks later, I was advised that I had been selected as a "Finalist." I was one of 30, still in the running for approximately 15 White House Fellows positions. We learned later that the commission had received over 6,400 applications for the fellowships. There were two reductions based on reviews of applications, after which 1,500 applicants were selected as Regional Finalists. Interestingly, of the 30 Finalists, seven were from the San Francisco Region. More than any other region! The San Francisco winners included David Lelewer, Stanford Law graduate and assistant to the Dean; Robert Haas, a Peace Corps member with a Harvard MBA; Richard Pascale, Stanford MBA and Assistant to the Dean of Admissions; Bob Joss, Stanford Ph.D. candidate; Larry Moss, a nuclear engineer with an MS degree; and Edgar Kaiser Jr., Stanford MBA, and economist with the A.I.D. I was surprised and thrilled beyond words to be in this esteemed group!

TO THE FINALS

In May, I set off for the Airlie House in Warrenton, Virginia: the heart of horse country, and site of the White House Fellows Finals. Airlie House is a lovely complex of buildings with attractive grounds and accommodations. My roommate was Major Jack Woodmansee, U.S. Army. Jack was a West Point graduate and a Vietnam veteran. At that time, he was an assistant professor at the U.S. Military Academy at West Point. He was a terrific "roomie," smart, with a great sense of humor and a positive attitude. We became best friends, and remain so to this day (Jack ended his career as a Lieutenant General).

The National Commission appointed by President Johnson was at Airlie House to select those who would be Fellows. It was a most impressive group. To mention just a few, Commission members included Douglas Dillon of Dillon Read and Company, and current Secretary of the Treasury; Olive Beech, CEO of Beech Aircraft Company; John Macy, Chairman of the Civil Service Commission; John Gardner, Secretary of Health, Education and Welfare; John Oakes, Editorial Page Editor for the New York Times; and William Friday, President of University of North Carolina.

The Finals were organized much like the Regionals, with interviews two-on-one. But now all three meals were with commissioners, which made for more interviews and poor indigestion. The cocktail hour presented a more casual and comfortable opportunity to talk and banter with the commissioners than the more formal after-noon interviews. Of course, all of the Finalists tried to "work the corners" with the commissioners. I was speaking with Olive Beech one evening, and noticed she had a small airplane pin in her coat lapel, certainly one of the Beech airplanes. She saw me looking at it. "That's a very nice pin," I said. "That's a Cessna Aircraft right?" Cessna was one of Beech's major competitors. She visibly stiffened and her smile disappeared. I had a hit a nerve. When she looked at me, I had a big grin on my face.

Once she realized that I was putting her on, she shook her finger at me and said, "I am going to remember you!" I quickly replied, "I hope so!"

After several full days and evenings of intense interaction with the commissioners, we were glad to be bussed back to Washington to the Civil Service Commission Building on E Street where the list of winners would be posted. We waited, for what seemed like eternity, in an office area. Needless to say, we were all nervous! When the list was finally posted, I was too far back to be able to read it. Edgar Kaiser, who was in front of me turned and told me that I was on the list. I didn't believe him until I saw it myself. Wow, I had won! And so had my roomie, Jack!

The 1968-69 White House Fellows, South Lawn of the White House. (I am 2nd from right, first row; Chuck Larson is to my right; Jack Woodmansee is 3rd to my right; Dave Miller is in back row, 6th from right)

I was later informed by someone present during the Commission's deliberations that Olive Beech told them if they didn't pick me as one of the winners, she would hire me herself!

MEETING THE PRESIDENT

On May 6th, the new Fellows were invited to a reception at the White House, where we would be welcomed by President and Mrs. Johnson, plus his cabinet officers! We were only a few blocks away, so the group walked. It was a beautiful spring day and spirits were high. We were admitted through the Southwest gate and went up the driveway. The entire first floor was involved in the reception, the U.S. Marine Orchestra was playing, there were several bars and many VIP's. The President received us in the State Dining Room. He was an impressive man to meet, 6'3" or so, with dark eyes behind thick glasses, and really big hands. When I shook hands with him, my hand disappeared in his. He pulled me close and stared down at me. It was disconcerting that I couldn't make out his eyes through his glasses. Quite the intimidation tactic!

I met many luminaries that night. Clark Clifford, Robert McNamara, Walt Rostow and Dean Rusk to name a few. It was heady wine indeed!

There was only one other new Fellow who was there without a wife. I had met Chuck Larson during the finals. He was a Lieutenant Commander in the Navy Nuclear Submarine Service and was first in his class at the Naval Academy. He and I were the first White House Fellows to be selected with just bachelor's degrees. We teamed up that evening and have been close ever since.

Chuck and I had a fine time (and lots of champagne) the night of the reception. In the course of the evening, we met the President's daughter, Lynda Bird. I don't remember what led up to it, but I drank champagne from her shoe! As the evening wore down, Chuck and I somehow found ourselves on the South Lawn with the President's dogs. About that time, the Secret Service politely invited us to leave. Years later, when I introduced my wife, Mary, to Lynda Bird, much to my amazement, she remembered the champagne and shoe incident and told Mary that she had "really big feet!"

Before we left Washington, we were asked our preference regarding assignments. I believed Richard Nixon would be the next president, and I wanted to be there. However, in casual talks with the new Fellows I knew that Edgar Kaiser was also opting for the White House. His father had been a major contributor to President Johnson's campaign, and I figured that he would get that assignment. I decided the next best assignment would be the Vice President's Office, so that's what I asked for and that's what I received. Edgar landed the White House assignment where he reported to Joe Califano, Johnson's Chief of Staff.

When he took office In January, 1969, President Nixon and his staff were not thrilled to have Edgar Kaiser Jr. in their midst! While the Fellows Program is not political, contending with the son of a major contributor to the competition's campaign was likely disconcerting. Behind the scenes, someone worked out a really smooth deal. Chuck Larson, my White House party buddy, had been assigned to the Department of the Interior. It was decided that Chuck would be brought to the White House as Naval Aide to the President, and Edgar would be transferred to the Interior Department. A perfect solution… although Edgar was probably not too thrilled. Chuck retired as a four-star admiral, having served as Superintendent of the Naval Academy and Commander in Chief of the Pacific Fleet. I am proud to be his youngest daughter Kirsten's Godfather.

LEAVING CALIFORNIA

A Washington real estate agent, Lila Burt Cummings, found a house for us to lease. At 4501 Macomb St. NW, it was just across the street from the Horace Mann Grammar School where the boys would attend school, and only a block from the American University at Ward Circle. It was a colonial-style brick, 2 stories with 3 bedrooms and 2 baths. It also had a full basement with a fireplace, no garage.

I returned to California to the plaudits of my friends and colleagues. Joan, however, was not thrilled. She loved her life where we were, and had read about Washington's wealth of protestors and riots, not to mention the tent village on the Mall, and that temperamental East Coast weather. I said it was a great opportunity for a year for all of us, especially the boys, to experience our Capitol City and environs. Bless her heart, she said "OK, fine. Let's go!"

In the mid-60s, Carrol Shelby, in cooperation with Ford, debuted the Shelby Cobra Coupe. We bought a 1968 model with a 528 cu.in. V-8 engine. The car was very quick. It had comfortable front seats, and two small seats in the back under the roll bar. After the moving company left, we climbed in the car, strapped the boys in the back and headed east. We spent about 10 days driving across the country, saw lots of places, and had a great time.

Before I asked Autonetics for a leave of absence, I sat quietly in my office one day, asking myself if the fellowship was really a good idea. I had been with the company 10 years and enjoyed an excellent reputation. I was a young manager in a division that had won a major contract and would have quality people working hard for years. On the other hand, I had been a manager for two years, and felt it was a good time to look at other possibilities. There were six managers in the Strike Division, and at least two of them were serious competition for the next step up: a director's slot. All of us, including the directors, had our eyes on the same prize, Vice President and General Manager of the division. I decided I wouldn't be going anywhere soon if I stayed, so why not take the fellowship and see what came of it? I asked for and received a one year leave of absence. I believe you should not be afraid of change. Stepping out of the orderly regimen of your career, and trying something new is an inspiring challenge, and one I welcomed. A life lesson.

A few days before we left, Leo Killen, my boss at the Strike Avionic Systems Division and a few of his more prestigious colleagues asked Joan and I to dinner at a lovely restaurant. They wanted to celebrate and send us off on a positive note. The night of the dinner, one of our boys was sick, and until he was better, we weren't going. Despite being a good two hours late, our hosts and their wives were very gracious. Joan and I certainly appreciated the thought behind the dinner.

HUBERT H. HUMPHREY

We were driving through Texas at the time of the Democratic National Convention in Chicago. I kept waiting for a call telling us to come to Chicago for the nomination process and all the associated festivities. My new boss and current Vice President of the United States, Hubert H. Humphrey, was running for President. Fortunately, I was told to continue on to Washington. Many of you may recall the unprecedented violence at the convention center and in the city about the Democratic Party Platform, President Johnson, Humphrey, and the war in Vietnam.

The moving van arrived in Washington, and we settled in to the new house. I reported for work in the Office of the Vice President, in the Executive Office Building (now the Eisenhower Office Building) directly across Executive Way from the West Wing in late September, 1968.

I was given a desk in an office with several staffers. It was clear to me that whatever experience I was in for, it was not going to be a traditional time in the Vice President's Office! Everything was election-oriented: staff, speech writers, politicos, friends, press, security ...it was pandemonium! My nominal boss through all this was the Vice President's administrative assistant, Bill Welsh. Bill was a good guy trying to do an impossible job.

I took a number of trips with the candidate, always on a chartered jet set up for political travel. There was a Press section, the candidate's private office, a staff area, guest seating, and an area set aside for communications. One trip was a swing through southern Texas: Houston, Harlingen, San Antonio and Dallas. From there we flew to Los Angeles, giving me a chance to see my folks.

Humphrey was a man of the people, but he had little discipline. For example, his staff lined up a one-hour TV session for him in San Antonio. It was the perfect opportunity for him to talk to people about the issues and make his case. Humphrey was animated, a good, albeit long-winded, speaker, and a natural for TV. However, on our way to the studio in the motorcade, Humphrey spotted several nuns waving on a corner. He ordered his limo to stop. Exiting with his security detail, he walked over to talk to the nuns. No one could pry him away! He ended up missing his TV time and a chance to speak to thousands. In the months that I was with him, that was characteristic.

THE HAPPY WARRIOR

Hubert Humphrey was a warm and outgoing individual. The Press nicknamed him the "Happy Warrior." President Johnson's staff tells the story that when Winston Churchill died in 1965, the President called Humphrey and told him that he wasn't going to send him to the state funeral in England. Humphrey asked him why not? The President said, "Because you are incapable of looking sad!"

I can't think of a better example of his personality than when Joan and I had a cocktail party at our home, and invited the Vice President and his wife Muriel, a wonderful lady. They joined in with our other guests and everyone enjoyed themselves. It was December, and cold, so guests had worn overcoats. When the Humphrey's were leaving and looking for their coats, our two boys, Howard and Paul, came forward with their coats... and a bill for checking them! They were charging .25 cents per coat. Without missing a beat, the Vice President reached into his pocket with a smile, and came up with the fee. Joan and I were chagrined to say the least! The Humphreys thought it showed "initiative" and laughed.

During the campaign, Richard Nixon gave a superb speech on his view of the presidency. The Vice President asked me to help write what his view would be. Along with his speech writers, I contributed what I thought he believed in and structured the White House organization to support it. When he gave the speech it was good. I was proud to be part of it, but it was not as good as Nixon's in my opinion. Hubert Humphrey had spent his entire Washington career in the Senate. Nixon, while he had been a Congressman, also had eight years of experience in the Executive Branch as Vice President under President Eisenhower. That experience showed in his vision of the presidency speech.

Humphrey brought his entire staff from the Senate (the legislative branch of government) to the executive branch when he became Vice President. It was a different world, but no one seemed to appreciate the fact. They'd brought their Senate mindset! There was little communication with LBJ's staff, and the two principals rarely talked. Thus, the President did not go out of his way to support Humphrey in the election.

AN ASSIGNMENT

One day, the Vice President asked me to come into his office. As I was the only business person on his staff, he asked me to do an analysis/study of what his White House organization should look like when he became President. I said I would be happy to do it, and he arranged access to LBJ's staff in the West Wing. I spent weeks interviewing and informally discussing the best ways for a president to organize his staff. What an experience! In addition to the interviews, I researched White House organizational philosophy and history, including the writings of Harvard's Professor Richard Neustadt among others. Clearly, the President's staff and structure should reflect his personal and political philosophies, and to complement his strengths and protect against his weaknesses. I believed he would especially need a strong chief of staff to manage his calendar and control access to the Oval Office. Some Administrations had done this more effectively than others. In any event, I recommended what I thought would best serve a President Humphrey.

The vice president and his chief of staff reviewed my report, and I responded to numerous questions. He complimented me on its thoroughness, and insights, and was genuine in his thanks. I very much enjoyed doing it, and was pleased that he liked it. That was the last time I had serious private time with him before the election.

"ACCESS"

Washington is an extremely socially-oriented city, and "access" to people of power is huge. In many ways it depends on who you know. I met a man named Tyler Abel through North American's Washington Office. Tyler was the Chief of Protocol for the State Department. His wife, Bess, was Lady Bird's Social Secretary based in the East Wing. The two of them virtually controlled "official entertainment." What a contact! Joan and I were invited to a number of events above and beyond the Fellows program activities, thanks to them.

LYNDON BAINES JOHNSON

Most mornings I walked across Executive Way from the Executive Office Building (EOB) to the double doors of the West Wing. In President Johnson's day, he had wire service machines such as UPI right at the entrance. It was fun to stand there reading the "happening" news from around the world. Occasionally, while I was standing there, the President would walk up and check the news. He typically said good morning, and after a pause, "Have you had your coffee?" Of course I would say "no" and he would invite me to the Oval Office. We entered and he would steer me to one of the two couches next to the fire place. A steward would appear with cups and coffee. Life was good!

We usually only had a minute or two before a secretary, Joe Califano, or an aide would come in. The President would get up and walk over to his desk, a good 20 to 30 feet away, and I was left to myself. I never knew when to leave. Often I just sat there taking it all in, watching the 3 television sets tuned into each of the major networks, or listening to whatever conversation or phone call was going on. Eventually I was always noticed and abruptly dismissed. It was a fascinating and unique experience!

There was another side to Lyndon Johnson. When he ran against Barry Goldwater, he carried the entire South…except the state of Alabama, which voted for Goldwater. To punish Alabama, he called Joe Califano into his office and told him to close the biggest federal employer in the state. Joe said he would look into who that would be. He came back shortly, and told the President that they could not close the largest federal employer in Alabama because it was NASA. The president said, "Well (expletive deleted) close the next biggest employer!" That turned out to be the Strategic Air Command's base in Mobile, Brookley Air Force Base. It had a 9600' runway, and employed over 12,000 people. The Air Force was told to close the base in 24 hours. They literally took broad axes to chop the cables powering machine tools so they could be ripped up and trucked out. It was an economic disaster for the city of Mobile. SAC moved their aircraft and equipment to Barksdale Air Force base in Louisiana.

AFTER THE ELECTION

Hubert Humphrey lost to Richard Nixon in November, 1968.

Everyone in the office of the Vice President was an appointee. Having lost the election, the staff packed up and left… except for me, the White House Fellow! Before January 20, 1969 when the new administration took over, I was at my desk, and the phone rang.

I answered, and a voice asked "Is this Hudson?"

"This is Hudson. How can I help you?"

"Bob Haldeman, calling from the Nixon Headquarters in the Pierre Hotel in New York." He was President Elect Nixon's Chief of Staff. His tone of voice was casual; like we had known each other for ages. I offered my congratulations for winning the election.

Bob said, "I understand that you wrote an organizational plan for the White House for Vice President Humphrey."

"Yes, I did." I said.

He asked, "Would you share it with me?"

Seeing no reason not to, I said "Sure."

"A secret service agent will pick it up. Thanks." He concluded.

That was certainly interesting, as I had no idea anyone outside Humphrey's immediate staff knew about my organizational plan, let alone Nixon's staff.

THE WHITE HOUSE FELLOWS YEARBOOK

One final comment on my Fellowship year. Having had a terrific time, I wanted to do something to "memorialize it." I decided to put together a yearbook for lack of a better phrase. From the Fellows Directors office, I gathered up pictures that had been taken over the year during our meetings and trips. I took them home and started to organize them into two groups. One section would be pictures of the Fellows taken during meetings, trips, and some candid shots. The other section would be a page or two on each Fellow, including a picture with his/her principal, and a good picture or two taken during the year. I also detailed our education program. At some point, reaching the conclusion that I needed help, I called Caro Luhrs. She was a medical doctor and our only female classmate. She agreed to help me and we managed to get it put together. Now, who could I get to print all 50 pages of it?

Long story short, I called Richard Helms, Director of the Central Intelligence Agency for a meeting. If you are wondering why he would take my call, never underestimate the power of a call placed through the White House Switchboard! I went to see him with all the material, explained what I was trying to do, and asked for his help. As you might suspect, his budget is classified. He has printing facilities, and no one would know anything about the C.I.A. printing our yearbook. He agreed. It was printed (at no cost to us) and I gave all my classmates copies. It was, of course, rather unique and a big hit with the Fellows. It was very helpful to me in writing about the program and our year in this biography as well. One thing I learned in my years in Washington, D.C. was to "think around corners." A life lesson.

President Eisenhower died on March 28, 1969. Joan and I were watching the late news on TV when it was announced. The announcement said that the President would lie in state in the Washington Cathedral. We got the boys up and dressed and drove to the cathedral to see the President. There were not many people there yet. It was dark except for a spotlight on the President's flag-draped coffin. There was an honor guard standing at the coffin as well. It was a very moving experience, even the boys were quiet. Ike was the first President I voted for once I became eligible to vote in 1956. RIP, Mr. President.

CHAPTER FOUR

The White House Fellows-Nixon Administration: 1969

We were fortunate to be able to attend many inaugural functions in addition to the President Nixon's swearing-in ceremony at the Capitol on January 20, 1969. One of the most notable was the Vice President's black tie event at the Smithsonian Institute on the Mall. The official group, of which Joan and I were part, gathered at the designated place on the side of the Mall across from the Portraits Gallery where the festivities would be held. We needed to cross the grass Mall; it was a good 300 feet. The difficulty with this was the wall of protestors on the Mall blocking our way. A dozen mounted Park Police formed a wedge around us, and we pushed across the Mall toward the Gallery. It was unbelievably frightening! Young people pressed against the horses, spitting, swearing and throwing things at us. The horses' flanks dripped blood, and the noise was awful. We all made it across but I don't think any of us will ever forget that night.

Shortly after January 20th, when the Nixon staff had moved into the White House, Bob Haldeman called me again. He asked me to come to his office in the West Wing. The large corner office that had been Joe Califano's in the Johnson Administration, just steps from the Oval Office. Bob was a UCLA graduate, sported a crew cut, a firm handshake and looked me straight in the eye. This was not a man to trifle with.

SURPRISE!

I was expecting him to ask about the organizational study I did for Humphrey, but instead he asked "What is this White House Fellows Program about? We are getting rid of a lot of programs that had built up over Johnson's term." I explained the program to him, emphasizing that it was non-political. I used myself as an example: that my wife and I had been the Republican Co- Chairs for Nixon for the city of Rosemead, California, and that this had been part of my application for the Fellows program. I said our class was made up of both parties, and I thought it was a good group. Excusing himself to talk to the President, he left the office. When he returned, he informed me, "The President said he would keep the program, if you will run it!" Well, that was certainly a shock. Staying another year was definitely not in my plans.

A meeting with H.R. Haldeman, President Nixon's Chief of Staff in his West Wing Office, 1969.

While we were discussing the program, I recommended that we re-instate the military. President Johnson had removed them from eligibility, ostensibly because the military could be considered "federal employees," but I thought Vietnam might have also been a factor in the decision. Bob agreed with including the military, but added that the President wanted fewer academics, and more businessmen.

This was clearly a critical time for the White House Fellows Program. The new administration was under no obligation to continue the program. If I said "No" it could very well end with us, the fourth class. I believed in the program, and thought it should transition from the Johnson to the Nixon Administration, and continue on into the future. I agreed to run the Fellows program for the next year.

Bob went on to say, "What do you want to do here?" I wanted to tell him that I would like to work for him, but thought the better of it.

What I did say was, "Put me wherever you think I can best contribute." He thought about if for a minute and said, "I think you should stay with Vice President Agnew, he needs you more than we do."

I never knew what, if any effect, my organizational study had on the Nixon White House. But, I came to find out that Bob had done an extensive study of White House organizations during the transition period at the Pierre Hotel (when he called me and asked for a copy of my study). He has been widely credited with creating the "staff system" of White House management that has prevailed in virtually every subsequent administration. Hmmm.

The next day or so, I was with the Vice President in the Cabinet Room when the President entered. Though there were a number of people present, I don't remember the occasion. The President picked up a pad from the table and said he was going to drop his middle initial (M for Milhous) from his official signature. He wrote "Richard Nixon" on the pad, put it down and proceeded out of the room. I caught Clint Hill's eye (he was on Agnew's security detail, more on him later) and nodded toward the pad. He leaned over and tore off the page with the signature, and gave it to me later. A fine memento!

SPIRO "TED" AGNEW

The Vice President's staff had now arrived in Washington from Baltimore. The Chief of Staff was a lawyer named Stan Blair. The staff politico was Art Sommer, the domestic affairs staffer was a young man named CD Ward and the newly appointed military attaché' was Army Brigadier General John (Mike) Dunn. Former astronaut Bill Anders was the Executive Secretary for the National Aeronautics and Space Council, which resided in the office of the Vice President. Stan Blair was my immediate boss.

I made the critical comment earlier, that Humphrey had brought all his staff from the Senate to the Executive Branch. I was disappointed to find that the former Governor of Maryland, Spiro Agnew, and now the Vice President, was bringing all his staff from Baltimore as well. For the eight or so months that I was involved, his staff and the President's did not connect, just as Humphrey's hadn't. I believe that the careful selection of staff is absolutely critical to the success of any principal. I don't see a difference between government and business in this regard! Transplanting an entire staff from one organization to another leaves no room for "blended integration" of the old and the new. "A fortiori" shows no interest in accommodation. A life lesson.

The White House is unique in many ways, but none perhaps as interesting as its payroll. There is, of course, a White House Budget, but it does not begin to show the number or cost of people working there. The reason it doesn't is because most of the staff are paid through a device called a "detail." For example, while I worked for the Vice President, I was paid by the Coast and Geodetic Survey, part of the Department of the Interior. My salary and expenses came from their budget. In other words, I was "detailed" from Interior to the Vice President's office. This is a long-standing practice in presidential administrations.

Early on in the Vice President's office, I met Clint Hill. He is most remembered, perhaps, as the secret service agent running after the President's open car following the shots in Dallas, and climbing over the trunk to cover Jackie Kennedy. He has since written several books about his service to five presidents. Clint was assigned to Agnew's security detail. Over time, as Joan and I participated in many of the Vice President's activities, we became friends.

Clint typically walked right behind the Vice President during events, hands behind his back. Whenever Joan would reach out to squeeze his hand in greeting, she'd comment that his hands were sweaty. Occasionally, we would join Clint and his buddies at the Rotunda Restaurant and Bar in SE Washington for drinks after work. Those were always fascinating conversations… and private.

THE "VEEP"

I liked my new boss, Spiro Agnew, "Ted" to his friends. He was well dressed, polite, and had a good sense of humor with a ready smile. His secret service detail liked him, which speaks volumes. Ted's wife, Judy, was very nice as well, but I didn't see her much during my time there. They lived in an apartment suite in the Sheraton Hotel in NW Washington (long before the Naval Observatory was made the Vice President's personal residence). The tempo of the office was much different from the frenetic campaign days with Hubert Humphrey.

As I have said, the Vice President's staff was also his staff when he was governor. They had all been together for a long time and didn't have much use for me, a newcomer. One person who understood my plight was General Dunn, "Mike." I spent a lot of time in his office along with the naval aide, Lieutenant Commander Les Palmer, talking about politics, the Washington Post, and local scuttlebutt. One day, I received a call from my dad. His brother, a retired major in the army, had passed away some time ago. His widow had recently told my dad that the military cemetery misspelled his name on the headstone, and she couldn't get anyone's attention to fix it. Was there anything I could do about it? I took it to Mike. Not only did he straighten out the headstone spelling, but ran a check on my uncle's pension and found that the widow was being underpaid! So she got a raise out of it as well! Goes to show that if you know who to ask, chances are virtually anything can be fixed! A life lesson.

The Vice President summoned me to his office in the West Wing one day. I noted that only he and one secretary were present, despite the fact that he had a larger office in the EOB, where his staff was located. Was he intentionally avoiding his staff? When I arrived he told me that he didn't think he was getting the right mail, and wanted me to look into it (confirmed, he was avoiding his staff). I said I would be happy to. Looking back, I should have realized right then that I couldn't do what he asked on my own recognizance. Sure enough, when I went to the top floor of EOB to the Vice President's mail room, I ran into the "lady in charge," Mary. She was, of course, from his staff in Baltimore. I couldn't invoke the Vice President's name without blowing my cover, so I tried to ask around about how his mail was separated; who decided what he would see and so forth. I got the hard stare, nothing doing Hudson! I was flummoxed. I felt bad, but had little choice other than to tell Stan Blair that the Vice President was concerned about what mail he was receiving, adding that I would be delighted to work the problem. Stan simply said, "Don't worry, I'll handle it." End of story.

MAKING A DIFFERENCE

I did, however make a lasting contribution to the Office of the Vice President. When I was working with Vice President Humphrey and his staff during the election, there were all kinds of people involved: permanent staff, temporary staff, staff from the Hill, political people, people from the Democratic National Committee, and whoever! How was all this paid for? The long story short is that other than the Vice President's salary and his secretary's salary, both of which are covered by the White House Budget, everyone is there as a detail. This means the Vice President has little control over the hiring and firing process, and no way to promote or give raises to his staff.

I went directly to Vice President Agnew and told him about my experience with Humphrey and his staff, and that I didn't think it made any sense. I asked his permission to approach the Bureau of Budget (BoB) and see if there wasn't something we could do about getting him his own budget. He approved.

I went to the BoB and started working my way through the many bureaucratic hoops. I made progress, to the point of needing legislation. I called the Vice President's Senate office manager, Walter Mote (the Vice President is also the President of the Senate) and asked for his help. We were successful, legislation was written and approved, and to this day the Vice President has his own budget! A lasting legacy, and a success I am proud of.

THE EDUCATION PROGRAM

There is another very important part of the White House Fellows experience besides the day to day job, as noted earlier. It's a wonderful education program, which is carefully conceived to maximize exposure to all aspects of the country, world leaders, and organizations. We met for lunches, dinners, cocktails, and briefings, not to mention tours and trips around the country. What we did in our year is far too much to relate here. Just a detailed description of the following two months ought to prove my point... Here's the itinerary for December, 1968 and July, 1969:

New York City trip, meetings with Thomas Watson, Chairman of the Board, IBM, President and Mrs. Lyndon

Johnson, Richard Helms, Director, Central Intelligence Agency, William Bundy, Assistant Secretary of State for East Asian and Pacific Affairs, F. Stone, Author and journalist, Clark Clifford, Secretary of Defense, Lawrence O'Brien, Chairman, Democratic National Committee, Meeting with, ex-drug addicts, ex-welfare recipients and black militants, Dean Rusk, Secretary, Department of State, Trip to Kennedy Space Center to view the launch of the first manned space trip to the moon, Apollo 8.

I have to comment on the launch of Apollo 8. It was truly an amazing experience.

Imagine: you wait along with the expectant crowd feeling the buzz, then, "T minus I" comes over the loudspeaker system. You begin to hear a low growl. Suddenly the grass is bending towards you, and you feel a hot wave of pressure on your face. The immense boom of the rocket engines hits you. The Saturn V with the Apollo Module on top slowly rises from the gantry, pushed upward by the brilliant plume of Apollo's thundering engines, vibrant against the blue sky. Cheers break out amongst the crowd and you find yourself cheering along, your voices drowned out by the overwhelming noise. Necks crane as you watch the Saturn V climb faster and faster upward, leaving huge white clouds of condensation in its wake.

The Apollo 8 was the first manned spacecraft to leave Earth's orbit, reach the Earth's moon, orbit it, and return safely to Earth. Frank Borman was in command, along with astronauts Jim Lovell and Bill Anders. It was magnificent!

Returning to the itinerary:

Melvin Laird, Secretary of Defense, Maurice Stans, Secretary of Commerce, Raymond Piles, Assistant Chief of Police, Winston Blount, Postmaster General, David Kennedy, Secretary of the Treasury, Arthur Burns, Counselor to the President, William McChesney Martin, Chairman of the Federal Reserve. Tour of the District of Columbia in police squad cars. Senator Edmund Muskie. Trip to Kennedy Space Center to view launch of Apollo 11. John Ehrlichman, Domestic Counselor to the President, Clifford Hardin, Secretary of the Department of Agriculture, George Schultz, Secretary, Department of Labor, Donald Rumsfeld, Director, Office of Economic Opportunity and Daniel Moynihan, Assistant to the President for Urban Affairs.

For one of the Fellows' more memorable meetings with a principal, we gathered at the State Department for a discussion and lunch with the Secretary, Henry Kissinger. There were about 20 of us in attendance. His Fellow introduced him, as was standard procedure for these kinds of events.

The introduction included information on where he was born, raised and educated. It included a long list of degrees, followed by a long list of honorary degrees, followed by a long list of international awards and accomplishments. Finally, he stopped and the Secretary stood up to speak in heavily accented English. "Vell, I vant to tank yu for dat vunderful introduction. My fahder vould haf been proud, and my mudder vould haf beleefed it!"

Every month was much like the above sample. We were really busy, both in our jobs and participating in the education program. Luckily, our wives and dates were often invited as well. Otherwise we might never have seen them!

WHITE HOUSE STAFF

One of the White House events my family and I really enjoyed, as a White House staff member, was being invited to the East Room Sunday Services initiated by President Nixon. They were well attended, not too long and always left you feeling positive about life... even when Billy Graham wasn't there!

Another "perk" associated with working at the White House was being able to come and go (with your White House Staff Badge of course). As an example, I took Joan Into the East Room late one night. We had the entire photographic exhibit of Ansel Adams to admire, just the two of us. The Secret Service was always there, of course, quietly in the background. Working there was an honor and privilege.

Meeting with President Nixon, Oval Office, 1969

Most everyone has heard of Camp David, named after President Eisenhower's grandson. The presidential country retreat is located on 130 acres of wooded hills some 65 miles north of the District of Columbia, in the Catoctin Mountains of Maryland. Technically, it is a military installation run by the Navy, and manned by both Navy and Marine Corps personnel. It began as a WPA (Works Project Administration) project under President Franklin Roosevelt (FDR) in the 1930's. FDR's doctors and friends encouraged him to find a place close to Washington, but far enough away to escape the pressures of the city. He orignially named the camp, Shangri-La.

I was fortunate to visit it several times, always by helicopter, courtesy of the Marines. The grounds were cool, shaded by large pine trees. The camp had secluded cabins and lodges, and featured a tennis court, movie theatre, bowling alley and hiking trails. It had all the modern conveniences, along with a state-of-the-art conference center. Over the years, many high ranking diplomats stayed there... Winston Churchill and Nikita Kruschev to mention just two. I thought it was just delightful.

The Navy had its Bureau of Weapons (BuWeps) located on the Mall, near the Washington Monument, close to where the Vietnam Memorial is today. It was a series of two-story wooden barracks-type buildings constructed during World War II. They were an eye sore. Every time the President's helicopter flew over them approaching the South Lawn of the White House, President Nixon would see them and each time, he would lean over and tell Bob Haldeman, "Get rid of them!" Still, it took almost 3 years to get it moved to Crystal City, Virginia and the buildings torn down. Just because you're the President doesn't mean what you want gets done... without persistent follow-up! Another life lesson.

PROTESTS

One night, I put on old but appropriate clothes and walked through heart of the protests. The National Mall had become a tent city, spilling around the Washington Monument and towards the Lincoln Memorial and the Tidal Basin. Unless you were actually, physically there it's hard to understand what an unbelievable sight that was! Hygiene was awful, trash everywhere, beards plentiful. There were no bras and little cover for the ladies. Marijuana and drugs were as prevalent as loud music and signs. A time not to be forgotten, and one, hopefully, never to be experienced again!

Another unforgettable event was when the staff was summoned to the East Room of the White House for a Secret Service Briefing in 1969. The briefing concerned what they were going to do if the Vietnam protesters came "over the fence" and onto the White House grounds. You cannot imagine a more apocalyptic atmosphere. The Secret Service stated they were "not going to do anything, until and unless protestors hit the doors to the White House." If they did, it would have been a major problem. I'll will leave it at that, and add thank God that never happened!

SECRET MISSION

Ed Goss, The vice President of North American Aviation's Washington, D.C. Office, called me in early May, 1969, with a request. The crew of APOLLO 10, Tom Stafford, Commander, Gene Cernan, Lunar Module Pilot, and John Young, Command Module Pilot, had asked for both the presidential and vice presidential flags to take with them on the mission. APOLLO 10 would be the first flight of an APOLLO Spacecraft to operate around the moon, including a Lunar Module descent to within 9 miles of the moon's surface and then rendezvous and dock with the Command Module. This was the "dress rehearsal" for APOLLO 11's landing on the moon, two months later on July 16, 1969.

The crew wanted to take the flags and then, present them to the president and vice president upon their return to Earth.

Ed wanted to know if I could get the flags. I told him that I could get the vice president's flag, but the president's was another matter. There was no way to do that without significant "inside" help. I decided that since this whole thing was "on the sly," the best way to go (probably the only way, short of getting arrested) was to enlist the help of the Secret Service. I went down to their basement offices in the White House. I explained the whole idea as best I could, and stressed that this was just "a loan." The flags would be returned to the principals upon successful completion of the mission. They agreed!

Before I gave the flags to North American, I took pictures of our boys, Howard and Paul, on the lawn in front of our house holding the flags. As we all now know, the mission was a great success. The crew was feted at the White House, and "after putting some miles on them" returned the flags to their respective owners none the worse for wear. It was really fun!

Howard and Paul holding the flags

As a family unit, we covered a lot of territory. We were able to visit many of the historic sites in Washington, D.C., including, among many others, the Smithsonian Air and Space Museum, old town Alexandria, Mount Vernon and Monticello, Gettysburg, the Chesapeake Bay, and the Naval Academy in Annapolis. We stayed at the latter many times with Chuck and Sally Larson when he was the Superintendent there. Then, such an exciting adventure! Now, wonderful memories.

Our Fellows year wrapped up in August with a Farewell Party at the National Portrait Gallery. It had been a really outstanding year! We had a great class of Fellows and enjoyed our year with them (and their wives and girlfriends) immensely. What a wonderful bond to share! While my year as a White House Fellow was coming to an end, my relationship with the program was continuing.

CHAPTER FIVE

The White House Fellows: Class of 1969-70

Sometime around June 1969, I began thinking about my new job as Executive Director of the Fellows Program. I moved into the program's suite of offices in the Civil Service Building on E Street, NW. Since I already knew the staff of four, settling in was not difficult.

EARLY TROUBLES

Initially, I focused on early planning, then spent some time looking into the workings of the program. To my dismay, I found that there was no money to run the education program for the coming year. When the program launched in 1964, John Gardner had reached out to foundations for grants to support the education program's needs, which included meals, cocktail parties, travel and related expenses. There were many supportive foundations, but the Carnegie Corporation, and the Rockefeller and IBM Foundations were the original principal supporters.

Fundraising from foundations was new territory for me, but there was no time to lose. I phoned the Rockefeller people in New York right away. They told me that while they had in fact provided "seed" money, they never intended to continue support for the Fellows Program. Once I told them my woeful tale, they kindly agreed to help out. When it was all said and done, I managed to get a number of generous grants for periods of three to five years from charitable and corporate foundations, such as the Olin Corporation.

While I'd secured sound financing going forward, I would have much rather spent that time and effort getting to know the new class of Fellows. But I'm pleased to have done the legwork that would support the education program for years to come!

One of the first things I did in my work with the Fellows was to schedule a three-day orientation meeting at the Airlie House in Northern Virginia. It was a superb opportunity for the Fellows to get to know each other in a comfortable environment, and for me to explain how things worked and what our plans were for the year.

THE CLASS

The class was a mix of races, backgrounds, educations, and political philosophies. The White House Fellows selection process, from the Presidential Commission to the Executive Director, was based on the Johnson administration's personnel and political philosophies. Nixon's people had had no "say" in the selection of this year's class. We probably would have seen a somewhat different collection of individuals had they been running it. As it stood, not everyone was happy about President Nixon's election, which is understandable in a group as diverse as the Fellows.

For the first time ever, the program had transitioned from a Democrat administration to a Republican administration, but the depth of support was fragile. In addition, there were concerns in the President's staff about the efficacy of the program. I reminded the new Fellows that we served at the "pleasure of the President," urging everyone to be very careful about what they said in public. Each needed to be as supportive of their respective principal as possible.

"If you cannot, in good conscience, support your principal, come and see me, and I will have you re-assigned." I followed up.

One of the Fellows had said that he was going to speak out against the President from the steps of the Capitol. For obvious reasons, a public attack on the President by a Fellow would be catastrophic for the entire program. I spoke privately with the two Fellows I feared posed the biggest threat. Fortunately, there were no major "public" breaches of protocol during the year, but there were several upsets within the administration that we were (fortunately) able to contain. The year greatly increased the rate at which my hair turned gray.

FOREIGN TRAVEL

When I reviewed the files on the new Fellows, one thing that popped out was that only one of them had ever been out of the country. As noted earlier, the military was not included this year, which was unfortunate. Having had four military officers in my class the previous year, I found that they brought maturity, experience and a sense of order that was very helpful, especially to the younger class members. I felt this class of Fellows needed exposure to the world outside the United States. They needed to see how other countries and people lived; taste their food and experience their customs. It would benefit them to experience how foreign governments differed from ours, and also learn how to socialize with foreign officials as well as citizens. If approved, it would be a first!

Easier said than done! How does one go about obtaining approval for such a Fellows trip? I knew our strength was in and around the White House, not the State Department or the Department of Defense. I decided to make an appointment with General Alexander Haig, Henry Kissinger's Deputy National Security Advisor.

I met him at his office in the basement of the West Wing. I explained the unique situation surrounding this year's Fellows. I suggested two trips: one to the Middle East, and the other to Western Europe. Each trip would have nine Fellows, for ease of management. He agreed to support us and I got busy making it happen.

I scheduled visits to Paris, Brussels, Rome and Berlin for the Western European Trip, and Cairo, Egypt, Tel Aviv and Jerusalem in Israel, and Amman, Jordan for the Middle Eastern Trip. Everyone involved from the U.S. Government, both at home and overseas, was superb in its support of us. And I didn't lose one single Fellow!

One of the most surprising meetings I had In the West Wing was with Daniel Moynihan, Assistant to the President for Urban Affairs. I was calling on him one morning to invite him to speak to the Fellows.

Daniel Moynihan was a very colorful person in the Nixon White House... and there weren't many. Much has been written about him, PhD, 3 term senator from NY, Ambassador to the U.N. and India, writer, sociologist/politician etc. One of my favorite quotes from him is, "The single most exciting thing in government is competence…because it is so rare."

I entered his office, introduced myself, and we shook hands. Other than "Good Morning," he asked, "Would you join me in a taste of Kentucky Mash"? I did, and he readily agreed to meet with the Fellows. A unique individual indeed!

MOVE TO VIRGINIA

In 1970, the ongoing protests and riots around American University, Ward Circle and environs finally convinced us it was time to leave Washington, D.C. One morning a large anti-war crowd gathered in Ward Circle, which was adjacent to our house and the American University. It had stopped traffic, including a Cadillac Limousine carrying Secretary of Defense Mel Laird. It was chaotic, complete with loud chanting and yelling… all nasty. I held Paul on my shoulders, standing at the curb so he could see. While we were standing there taking it all in, a rock struck the tree right next to Paul's head. That was the last time we went out during a protest. Shortly thereafter, Joan and I decided to move from Washington. D.C., to Virginia.

We leased a house in Arlington, Virginia, just off Spout Run on Lincoln Street. It was a nice bungalow with a pool.

CHILDRENS' HOSPITAL

When our youngest son, Paul, was born, he was diagnosed with "aortic stenosis." This means a narrowing or stricture of the aorta, the largest artery in the heart. The doctors had told us that he would most likely need surgery to repair it in eight to ten years.

Now, in the middle of my first year as Director of the White House Fellows Program, it was time.

We were referred to a pediatric cardiologist, Lew Scott, and a cardiac surgeon, Mac McClanathan. Both of them worked out of Children's Hospital in the District. They were great with Paul, and the surgical repair of the aorta went just fine. However, when Dr. Mac was doing the repair, he noticed that Paul's aortic valve was bi-cusped, and it should have been tri-cusped. This meant that when Paul was 45 to 50, he would most likely need an artificial aortic valve. In the meantime, he would be fine, and we were happy!

WHITE HOUSE SWITCHBOARD

After our class finished the fellowship year, my roomie, Jack, was ordered back to Vietnam for another tour. This time to command an Air Cavalry Squadron. I drove him to Dulles Airport and saw him off.

On several occasions during the next months, I would call the White House Switchboard and ask them to find Lt. Col. Jack Woodmansee in Vietnam. That is all the information I had on Jack, and no one asked me for more. Within four or five minutes, my phone would ring and the operator would say, "I have Col. Woodmansee for you."

"Hello, Jack?" Then some static.

Jack would say, "Hud, do you realize who much fuss you cause when everyone hears that the White House is on the phone for me?"

"I don't care, Jack, how the hell are you?"

We would chat for a few minutes and he would tell me that he is getting his mail, everything was going fine, and to please give his love and hugs to Patty and the kids. I always enjoyed calling Patty, and telling her I just spoke with Jack, and he's fine.

I don't know how often the switchboard called Vietnam. I suspect General Westmoreland got plenty of calls. But those ladies knew what they were doing, and to them Jack was just as important as anyone else. I have no idea how they worked their magic to find him, but they did. I know it meant a lot to both of us, and to his family.

CLASS OF 1970-71 SELECTIONS

About this time, applications for the White House Fellows Class of 1970-71 were coming in, hundreds a week! I had far too much going on in the office to concentrate on reading applications, so, I would bundle them up and take them home. I had a room set aside where I could read and concentrate. I don't know how my predecessor reviewed the applications, but I had a straight forward system. After carefully reading the entire application, essays and all, I made three piles. One for "strong," one for "possible," and one for "weak." The biggest pile by far was the "possible."

I looked at background, education, experience (both life and job), achievements, community and professional involvement, and searched for insights into his or her personality. At this point in the process, it was only the paper application I had to work with. After a year as a Fellow, and another year running the program, I believe I had a good "sense" or "feel" for a promising Fellow.

I especially wanted a good group of semi-finalists for the regional reviews, and a strong representative pool of 30 finalists from which the new national commissioners would select.

BEYOND THE FELLOWSHIP

In late spring of 1970, my company called and asked what my thoughts were on returning to work (after all, they had extended my leave of absence another year). I told them that I planned on returning at the end of the fellowship year that I was managing, probably in the summer. The company said that one of their divisions, Textile Machine, was looking for a vice president of marketing. Would I go and interview? The division was located in Wyomissing, Pennsylvania, close to Reading. I felt I had to go, even if I had no desire to work there.

The President of the division was Ralph Ytterberg. The division manufactured panty hose machines, surgical needles, owned the Rimaldi Sewing Machine Company in Europe and, 10,000 acres of hardwood lumber in the North East. I still have no idea how the company's request tied into my ten years of defense electronics experience.

Harry Flemming, a friend and the White House personnel guru, somehow heard that I was looking to leave the government and called me. "We don't want you to leave, what can we do to keep you?" He mentioned several possibilities, but nothing of interest. He called back with some intriguing news. The President had opened a new office in the Department of Transportation, the Urban Mass Transit Authority (UMTA).

"Would you be interested in the director position?"

"Hmmm, maybe!" I had always seen the potential in mass transit, especially growing up in the Los Angeles area during the "red cars" era.

"Yes, I would like to look into the opportunity."

I went over to the Department of Transportation, and was met by their personnel people, who took me to a new suite of offices on the top floor. It had a very nice view of the city. I was introduced to the small staff of five or six and shown around.

"What's the plan and how much is your budget?" I asked.

A long silence. "Uh, there is no budget other than payroll."

End of interest. In Washington, money is everything. With money you can do something positive; you have influence. Without money, you have zip. When the President asks, and Congress funds an urban mass transit initiative, call me. Until then? No thank you!

The Regional Finals were over, and I had selected the 30 Finalists who would be invited to Airlie House for meetings with the new National Commission. I had also been thinking of someone to take my place as Executive Director. A friend who came quickly to mind was David Miller, a Fellow 68-69 classmate. He was young, well spoken, bright, and had an engaging personality. David held a University of Michigan law degree. He also lived in town with his delightful wife, Molly! He and I discussed it a number of times, and he agreed the most opportune time to take over the program would be when the new National Commission gathered at the Airlie House for the final selection process. The timing was perfect.

CHAPTER SIX

The United States Department of Commerce 1970-1972

Several weeks later, I got a phone call from Rocco Siciliano, the Under Secretary of Commerce. He was the number two official in the department, under the Secretary, Maurice Stans. He was looking for a deputy, and heard I might be interested. Would I like to talk to him about it?

"Yes, I would."

We met and talked several times and he offered me the position. Now, the hard part: talking with Joan. She had not wanted to come to Washington for even one year! But she did. I hadn't even consulted her when Bob Haldeman and the President asked me to run the Fellows program, committing us to another year. Now, we were looking at another year or two, minimally. Joan and I discussed it at length, including the possible effects on the boys, and on my career. She agreed that it would be a good thing for us. So, I accepted the appointment as Deputy Under Secretary of Commerce. I was 35 years old.

Deputy Under Secretary of Commerce, 1970

My folks and my brother flew in from California and Texas, respectively, for the swearing-in by the Secretary of Commerce, Maurice Stans. I was thrilled that they came. It was an impressive ceremony. No one in the family had ever served in Washington, D.C., and we all had a fine time celebrating afterwards.

There were many aspects to the job. One of my favorites was being Chief of the U.S. Delegation to the Organization for the Economic Cooperation and Development, Industry Committee (OECD), in Paris, France. I was also the Commerce Department's Delegate to the International Labor Organization, ILO, in Geneva, Switzerland along with the State Department's delegate.

In the transfer from the White House to Commerce, I kept my diplomatic passport, a privilege I loved. You could walk through customs/immigration like a stroll in the park. The OECD Meetings were laborious, but provided interesting exposure to an international organization and the political interplay between foreign delegations. The food and wine of Paris and Geneva were a terrible hardship as well!

Washington is a fascinating place. Its structure is built on who has power, whether real or perceived...quite a distinction! Here is a fun example.

During a reception one night, I met the Vice President of Goodyear Rubber Co.'s Washington Office. He learned of my interest in Formula One and Grand Prix Racing. On my next trip to Europe he arranged for me to meet a famous racing photographer, Bernard Cahier, who was also Goodyear's representative for European Gran Prix Racing.

When I had a trip to Europe, I would advise Bernard and he would take me to a race or a track where cars were being tested, or shops where the cars were meticulously built by hand.

In the early 1970s, the U.S. was imposing "padded safety bumpers" on automobiles, in lieu of the old chrome steel bumpers. European sports car manufacturers were scared to death of having those ugly bumpers imposed on their beautiful cars.

Bernard, it seems, gave them the message that I was a key player in the bumper decision process in Washington. Can you imagine? Well, perhaps I didn't dispute it much!

Let me tell you, the effect was quite amazing. When I came to Europe I had my choice of cars: Porsche Carrera, or several varieties of Mercedes Benz. I toured both the factories and company race tracks for Porsche and Ferrari, and had lunch with the leadership. I also got a ride in a racing Porsche 914 around the famous Nurburgring in Germany. Scary!

MEETING ENZO

Enzo Ferrari was an interesting man. When I had lunch with him, he ate a plate of plain pasta with a little cream sauce on it, and talked about his latest F-1 machine. Jacky Ickx, the famous Belgian driver sat at the next table with the other drivers, or "pilots" as they called them. After lunch we went to the track where the drivers were putting the cars through their paces. Enzo sat in a darkened room with TV screens on the walls, quietly watching his cars race through the turns and straights.

Needless to say, neither I nor the Commerce Department had any say in the safety bumper issue, but I sure enjoyed the ride!

SOME INVITATIONS

During my time as Deputy, the White House asked me to represent the President at Romania's first International Trade Fair, in Bucharest. I stayed with our Ambassador and met the President of Romania, Nicolae Ceausescu. In addition to the Industrial Trade Fair, I visited the Ploesti Oil Fields (the scene of massive bombing in WW2), and the lovely Carpathian Mountains.

I was also invited to be the U.S. Government's representative at the opening of the Sheraton Hammamet Hotel in Tunisia. It was a black tie event, but no one had told me that. I had a Brooks Brothers narrow blue and white stripe summer weight suit and a dark blue tie with me. I just told everyone that this was a "California Tux" and fought to keep a straight face!

I had a beautiful suite at the hotel overlooking the Mediterranean Sea. In the morning, I ordered room service and it was served on my deck. I asked for a boiled egg, toast and coffee. When the waiter delivered my breakfast and set everything up, I stared at my egg sitting up in a little cup... still in its shell! I had no idea how to eat it, all I had was a small spoon. Was this a mistake or what?

My foreign food experience had all been in the Pacific area, and I had never seen anything like this. Since no one was looking, I smashed the egg on my plate, removed the shell as best I could, and ate it. I have since learned the proper etiquette in such situations!

Back in the Commerce Department, I attended the Secretary's weekly staff meetings. All I remember of them is that every week he would ask what the status was of the McDonald's franchise for his son?

MEET THE BUREAUCRACY

I also agreed to run the Bureau of Domestic Commerce (BDC), an organization of some 350 people. Much of what it had been doing for years was way out of date. For example, worrying about machine tools from the Korean War!

BDC was a very staid, bureaucratic organization, and not particularly receptive to new ideas and initiatives from political appointees. It was impossible to dismiss anyone. If they did not want to do what you or the administration wanted, there was little you could do, other than trying to convince them of the merits of your case. With some it worked, with others it did not. It was an education.

What I ran into was nothing new... In 1952, Dwight Eisenhower was elected President. His predecessor, Harry Truman opined that he would quickly learn that a general has more power than a president. "Poor Ike," said Truman. "When he was a general, he gave an order and it was carried out. Now, he's going to sit in that big office and he'll give an order and not a damn thing is going to happen."

I invited John Ehrlichman, Assistant to the President for Domestic Affairs, to come over from the White House and speak to my staff about current issues and events of interest. He came on several occasions and spoke with candor. It was a huge hit with my staff,

I was able to hire some excellent people, and we opened a Policy Office to review current and future business trends. We established industry financial analyses, including the services sector as well as an office to look at "franchising." We built an effective legislative group, made the Commerce Field Offices more responsive to the business community, and installed a management information system.

To help me with the new initiatives, I called a former Fellow, Dick Ramsden, who lived in New Hampshire. He had an astute financial mind and I thought he could help me get things going in the department. When I called, and asked him him to be a consultant (offering $175.00 a day), he said, "OMG! do you realize all the paperwork I would have to fill out regarding my financial holdings?" I begged and Dick agreed, good fellow that he was. Dick did all the paperwork, and was approved as a consultant. He came down to Washington and we spent several days working on establishing a franchising office in the department. Things were going great.

RE-CONNECTING

Since I had taken my leave of absence from Autonetics for the White House Fellows, my old boss Leo Killen, had left the company. He had taken a position with Teledyne Inc., a conglomerate based in Century City, California. Leo headed up Teledyne's European and Middle Eastern Offices out of his base in Geneva, Switzerland.

The next time I went to Geneva for an ILO meeting, I called Leo and made arrangements to get together for drinks and dinner.

It was great fun getting caught up with him after a long hiatus, discussing the "goings on" at Autonetics and North American Aviation while I had been on leave. I saw a lot of Leo and his lovely wife, Danielle during my visits to Geneva. We played golf at their beautiful Geneva Country Club, and had delightful dinners at the Richemond Hotel and other nice places around Lake Geneva.

Leo's big story, briefly, was that North American was set to take over the Rockwell Corporation after I left on leave. However, North American failed to disclose an overrun on the MK II Program of some $32 million dollars. That disclosure changed the representation on the board between the two companies, and Rockwell ended up taking over North American! It was now the North American Rockwell Corporation, with corporate offices in Pittsburgh, Pennsylvania. The change had no direct impact on me or my leave of absence, but it sure didn't say much for my return to the company.

I received another phone call from the White House Personnel Office. John Eisenhower, the former president's son, was retiring from his post as Ambassador to Belgium. Would I be interested? There was a lot to be said for that ambassadorship. It would be an outstanding European experience for the boys, replete with history, the arts, good schools, and of course, soccer. For Joan and I there would be a great social scene, political intrigue, new friends, and first class cuisine and wines. Brussels was "the" financial center of the continent. A couple of years there would help me establish excellent credentials for a position in New York or Washington, D.C.! Needless to say, that opportunity was "dead on arrival" at home.

A PHONE CALL FROM THE WHITE HOUSE

As I said earlier, things were going great at Commerce… until they weren't. I got a phone call from Peter Flannigan. Peter was one of the few Assistants to the President, along with the likes of Kissinger, Haldeman, and Ehrlichman.

"I understand that you have Dick Ramsden as a consultant, right?" Peter queried.

"Yes, I do."

"I would like to borrow him on a detail." Peter said. You remember what that means: I pay; he benefits. I agreed, because that's what you do when the White House calls. I hoped for Dick's early return, but who knew?

Perhaps a month or two later, there was a huge splash in the Washington Post newspaper about an ITT Corporation scandal, involving Ms. Dita Beard who was one of the company's lobbyists in town. It had to do with the company's planned divestiture of one of its divisions, and possible inappropriate executive branch interference with the process. These things happened all the time in Washington, I didn't pay much attention. Until I did!

All of a sudden, I started getting phone calls from the Attorney General's office. John Mitchell, President Nixon's Attorney General (AG), had resigned. I don't remember if it was when he took over the Committee to Reelect Nixon in March 1972, or in July after the Watergate break-in. The problem was that his deputy, Dick Kleindeinst, was up for confirmation in the Senate for Attorney General… but the confirmation was being held up in committee because of the ITT business. Uh oh!

The calls I received from Kleindeinst's staff were awful, both in message and in language. They wanted me to say that I knew my consultant, Dick Ramsden, was working on the ITT issue for Peter Flannigan in the White House. They believed that this information would help get Kleindeinst's confirmation cleared. I had no idea what Dick Ramsden was doing there, none! This made no difference regarding the threatening calls I was getting, but no way was I going to lie about it. Joan was getting nasty calls at home as well. It got so bad that I suggested she stop answering the phone.

POLITICS

When Secretary Stans, finally called he said, "Hudson, regarding this issue with the Justice Department... you are on your own."

What? I couldn't believe it.

I was being abandoned politically. None of our friends called either. When there is blood in the water, everyone goes to ground. I told Joan that "we could be fired." How disappointing that would be after all the wonderful things that had happened to us as a Fellow and White House Staff member over the last two years.. I had no idea what to do, other than having a few stiff Scotch on the rocks. We held out for another day.

I was getting ready to call Bob Haldeman at the White House and ask for help, when suddenly, the whole thing broke. Whoever was sitting on Kleindienst's appointment to AG in the Senate, released it. In moments, the whole thing blew over, like nothing had happened. Washington is a beautiful city, the streets are organized: numbered streets run north and south, lettered streets run east and west, and avenues are free spirits. But it is primarily a political city. It can, and does, chew people up and spit them out. I was lucky.

Secretary Stans left the Commerce Department in February, 1972 to chair the Finance Committee for the Re-Election of President Nixon. He was replaced by Peter G. Peterson, a businessman and investment banker who went on to make a fortune later in his career as co-founder of the Blackstone Group. Peter was much more personable than Stans, and the whole department "lightened up" under his leadership. We got along great.

Joan and I decided it was time for us to get back to the private sector. Four years in Washington was enough. When I was in Geneva the next trip, I told Leo that I was going to leave government. He said, "I'll call George Roberts, the CEO of Teledyne, and set you up for an interview."

GOING WEST

In early 1972, Dr. Roberts called and invited me out to Los Angeles for a visit. We met in his office on Avenue of the Stars in Century City, the old MGM lot. We talked about many things, including my background, what I wanted to do and so on.

I said I did not want to go back into aerospace. "OK," he said, "I want you to go to San Diego and see Bill Rutherford, our Pacific Group Executive." I flew down to San Diego in the company King Air with Bob Schwanhausser, Teledyne Ryan Aeronautical's Vietnam drone expert.

I was introduced to Bill in his office, immediately adjacent to the San Diego Airport. He looked after 12 or so Teledyne companies, located from San Diego up to San Francisco. Virtually all defense companies! Reviewing my resume, he said, "UCLA, educated with the masses, eh?" I bit my tongue. It turns out Bill was a Stanford graduate and also from the law school. All three of his kids went to Stanford, including one son who went to its medical school.

TRE

The next morning I was taken to the Teledyne Ryan Electronics (TRE) Division, 30 minutes north off HIghway 163 in Clairemont Mesa. The electronics company had designed and built the landing radar for the APOLLO 11 flight to the Moon. It also had just received the contract to design and build the landing radar and space alitimeter for the VIKING Mission to Mars.

Teledyne was looking for a new VP General Manager because the incumbent, Dick Iverson, had quit and gone to work for General Dynamics Electronics. Interestingly, Dick was a Vice President. However, the job they were offering me added an important designation... General Manager. Hmmm? In the interim, Charley Badewitcz, a former navy pilot and engineer, was managing the division. Apparently, Teledyne did not think he was the man for the job.

The division's non-space business was defense oriented, designing and manufacturing Doppler Radar Sensors for Navy helicopter navigation. It had one radar in production, the APN 182 ("A" for aircraft, "P" for radar, and "N" for navigation, in military parlance) for the SH-2 and SH-3 Navy helicopters. The other product was a development effort, the APN 200: the first solid state radar for the Navy's S3A aircraft. The division occupied one half of a 300,000 square foot facility. The other half was leased to the Digital Data Corporation. TRE had about 170 employees, and the UAW. Sales were about $7M.

AN OFFER

We met again the next morning, and Bill offered me the Vice President and General Managers position at Ryan Electronics.

Leo Killen must have said some really good things about me! I said I would talk to my family and get back to him. I returned to Washington.

Ryan Electrics was offering a salary of $40,000 a year and a company car. I was disappointed with the salary, but after talking with Joan, decided not to counter. We were going back to California... San Diego, nonetheless. We could look forward to great weather, and living reasonably close to both of our parents. I'd be filling my first Vice President-General Manager's position. What's not to like? I notified North American that I would not be returning from leave. My pension for the ten years I was with them was secure.

The family felt San Diego would be fine. I accepted the offer, we put our Orange County home (which we had leased while we were in Washington) on the market, and started making plans for the move. So much for not wanting to work in the defense industry!

In looking back on my decision to take the fellowship, and give up my position at Autonetics, it is fair to say that I would never have made Vice President and General Manager at Autonetics (or with North American for that matter) in four short years. The Fellowship and ensuing positons with the Administration in Washington, D.C. was a miraculous segue! Another life lesson.

The Commerce Department threw a big party for me on the building's top floor veranda. All the "brass" attended and the view overlooking the South Lawn of the White House as the sun set was, as always, inspiring. It was a productive and exciting two years. I grew from the experience and made many friends around the world, for which I am forever grateful.

THE WHITE HOUSE

WASHINGTON

The Western White House
San Clemente

August 28, 1970

Dear Hudson:

This is just a note to tell you how pleased I have
been by the great energy and dedication that have
marked your work with the Commission on White
House Fellows. You deserve to feel a great
sense of pride as you leave this assignment and
I am glad this Administration will continue to
benefit from your great talent and initiative in
the Department of Commerce.

With all good wishes for success and with my
appreciation and best wishes,

Sincerely,

Richard Nixon

Honorable Hudson B. Drake
Deputy Under Secretary of Commerce
Department of Commerce
Washington, D. C.

Letter from President Nixon, 1970

I have two final comments on the Nixon Administration and the war in Vietnam. The President brought the war to an end. He also held the largest White House Dinner Party in history, by tenting the entire South Lawn, and inviting all the Vietnam POW's and their wives to dinner. Over 1,000 guests!

President Nixon always treated me professionally, and it was an honor to be member of his staff. RIP, Mr. President.

Bob Haldeman was a big help to me. With his and the President's assistance, we had "saved" the White House Fellows Program in its first major change of administrations, and made it available to future generations. A legacy to be proud of! Bob also gave me the latitude to run the White House Fellows Program and the selection process without undue hindrance from the White House Staff. RIP Bob.

My thanks also to John Erlichman, who was never too important to come and "talk to the troops." RIP John.

THE WHITE HOUSE
WASHINGTON

September 6, 1972

Dear Hudson:

The outstanding job you have done at the Department of Commerce is appreciated by all of us at the White House.

My best wishes go with you as you and your family leave the Administration for your new position with Teledyne Ryan Aeronautical.

Sincerely,

H. R. Haldeman
Assistant to the President

Mr. Hudson B. Drake
Deputy Assistant Secretary
   and Director
Bureau of Domestic Commerce
Department of Commerce
Washington, D. C.   20230

Letter from Bob Haldeman, Chief of Staff

THE WHITE HOUSE

WASHINGTON

January 9, 1971

Dear Hudson:

You were very thoughtful to send me your note of
January 5, 1971 commenting on the White House
Fellow's smash trip to South America. It would
be a travesty were I to attempt to take credit for
a project which was spawned and bore fruit under
your tutelage and as a result of your energy and
drive.

All this said, it was nonetheless a rewarding
experience to watch this year's group of Fellows
perform with perfection before the President.
They were indeed a credit to all the work you
did last year and the President commented to me
after the meeting that he was especially impressed
by the soundness of their views and the maturity and
skill with which they expressed themselves.

Best wishes,

Alexander M. Haig, Jr.
Brigadier General, U. S. A.
Deputy Assistant to the President
for National Security Affairs

Honorable Hudson B. Drake
Deputy Under Secretary
Department of Commerce
Washington, D. C. 20230

Letter from Alexander M. Haig, Jr.

THE WHITE HOUSE
WASHINGTON

September 14, 1972

Dear Hudson:

Thanks so much for your letter which arrived in my absence.

I am delighted for you that you have found so interesting a challenge in the private sector. At the same time I regret the Administration's loss since it was always a matter of considerable pride and comfort to know that you were such a steadfast and active part of the team.

I very much enjoyed our association and look forward to seeing you in San Diego.

Congratulations on a job well done.

Kindest personal regards.

Yours sincerely,

John D. Ehrlichman
Assistant to the President
for Domestic Affairs

Mr. Hudson B. Drake
18047 Sencillo Drive
San Diego, California 92128

Letter from John Erlichman

CHAPTER SEVEN

Teledyne Ryan Electronics
1972-1984

Books have been written about Henry Singleton and the formation of Teledyne. For the purposes of this book, a brief commentary regarding Teledyne's beginnings and philosophy would be useful to the reader. Since I spent 25 years with the company, this short history will hopefully assist in understanding some of the things I did or in which I was involved.

Dr. Henry Singleton (PhD in Electrical Engineering) and a colleague left Litton Industries together and started Teledyne in 1960. Singleton believed the company's success lay in the semiconductor business, the "basic building blocks of electronics," and that this success would lead to other high technology and high growth inventions. He briefly attended the Naval Academy with George Roberts (PhD in Metallurgy). There they became friends and stayed in touch over the years. While Henry was busy buying companies in the semiconductor field, George was building a company called Vasco Metals Corporation, which specialized in vacuum melted alloys such as nickel and titanium. In July of 1966, the companies merged, marking Teledyne's entry into the high tech metals business. Henry was named CEO and George was president. Teledyne was growing both physically and financially, primarily through acquisition of companies.

One of the company's hallmarks was the unique and comprehensive financial reporting system that they developed. Each company within Teledyne prepared an annual capital budget, referred to as Profit Plan 1, which was the company's business plan for the year. In five months or so, an updated plan was prepared: Profit Plan 2.

Reports on these plans were provided to corporate monthly. For the approval of the Profit Plans, company presidents and key staff went to the corporate offices and made presentations. Individual controllers of each company reported to the company president and the corporate controller at the end of each month, facilitating timely and accurate quarterly and annual reports.

For much of its history, a basic element of the company's operating philosophy and one of its core strengths was each local company president's autonomy. I have long believed that the best job in Teledyne was that of a company president. Teledyne gave the president the power and authority to run his company with the resources of a major corporation backing his endeavors. The president enjoyed limited interference by the corporate staff as he worked to implement his plans. He was allowed to run the show in terms of day-to-day decision making and in setting long term strategies. The *one* requirement was that he "make his numbers."

In the summer of 1972, we arrived in San Diego after an uneventful drive across the country. The company put us in a motel in Rancho Bernardo, roughly 30-40 minutes north of the TRE facility just off Interstate 15.

We were originally scheduled to stay at the Rancho Bernardo Inn, an upscale resort that featured a swimming pool, among other amenities. The boys would have enjoyed this immensely! For some reason someone at the company changed the reservation during our drive, moving us to a nearby motel that had absolutely nothing. To this day I wonder who did that to us...

COMING HOME TO SAN DIEGO

We started house hunting immediately and worked our way through a number of San Diego areas. We liked the country at-mosphere of Ranch Bernardo and focused our search there. We found a new home on the private Rancho Bernardo Golf Club and made an offer. It was a four bedroom, three bath two-story house at 18047 Sencillo Drive, which was at the top of a hill. It had great views and a nice breeze. I estimate that it had about 3000 sq. ft., and our purchase price was $74,000.

If you went down the street and turned right, you were on Pomerado Road. Across from it was "open space" for miles. When I looked at all of that open space, I saw an opportunity to bond with the boys, which seemed especially important after four years in D.C. I wanted to teach them something about basic mechanics and caring for a machine, so we bought three dirt bikes: a Honda 75cc for Paul, a 125cc for Howard, and a 250cc for me.

It was illegal, of course, for the boys to ride on public streets, but it wasn't far to the dirt. The three of us really had fun times roar-ing around the back-country. One day, after finishing our ride, we drove onto Pomerado Road and headed the 100 yards or so to our turnoff street for home. No sooner were we on the street than a cop car drove by going the other way. Pomerado was divided by a median, so when he saw us he had to keep going until he could make a U-turn at a break in the median. When he hit his lights and took off, so did we…in the opposite direction! We "hauled ass" to the turn and headed up our street, full bore.

We got to our house at the top of the hill and up the driveway. Howard yanked up the garage door and we zoomed in. He slammed the door shut just as the cop drove by looking for us. Whew! That was close…but great fun! So much for setting examples for your kids! Sometime later, Paul collided with another bike and broke his femur. He spent months in the hospital, effectively ending the dirt bike era.

The Dirt Bike Trio (left to right - Howard, me and Paul). Rancho Bernardo, 1972-3

GETTING STARTED

When I arrived at TRE I set up my office and went about meeting my new employees. Since we were a division of Teledyne Ryan Aeronautical, I was a Vice President-General Manager, and my top line people were directors (as opposed to president and vice presidents). Most of them had been at TRE for a number of years and appeared happy in their work.

TRE was a "microwave house" which encompassed aircraft navigation equipment. We dealt with high frequencies in our radars; our one and only product. These radars operated at 13.3 Ghz (thirteen point three billion cycles per second). Our radars operated on the Doppler Effect, which is the pseudo shift in frequency due to "movement." A good example of this is the whistle on a moving train. If you were standing on the platform of the train station, you would hear the train's whistle as it approached. It would seem to become higher in frequency (louder) as the train grew closer, and lower in frequency (quieter) when it passed. If you were on the train, the whistle's frequency would have remained constant. It is this "apparent" shift in frequency that is known as the Doppler Effect, or shift.

Stay with me for one more paragraph! TRE's Doppler Radar Navigation Systems functioned on that same basic principle. The radar antenna radiated (projected) four very narrow beams of microwave energy at the ground. The position of these beams was precisely known as to their pointing angles and beam widths. The reflected energy from these beams, bouncing back to the aircraft from the ground, was amplified, processed by the radar frequency tracker, and sent to its computer. The computer then translated the data into aircraft velocity, or speed.

The navigation system required an Aircraft Heading Reference System which consisted of a magnetic heading (compass) and three-axis gyro system. When the radar's antenna was corrected to the actual attitude of the aircraft, as determined by the relationship between the axis and a reference datum such as the horizon, the aircraft velocity vector (direction or course) was then available for navigation of the aircraft. In other words, you knew the speed of the aircraft, the direction you were going, and your starting position (latitude/longitude), so you were then able to "navigate."

As the new leader, I essentially had two jobs. One was to learn about microwave and our products: what was being developed, and for whom. The second was to deal with a very important, no, critical customer, the Martin Company. The Martin Company was the prime contractor on the VIKING Mission to Mars. Our contract was for the space altimeter and the landing radar. When I arrived we were behind schedule due to technical problems, which in turn, caused overruns to the program's budget and schedule delays. The customer's program manager, Bill Purdy, had called for Saturday meetings until we solved our problems and got back on schedule. Easier said than done! It took two years of really hard work to get it done, but we did!

THE CABAL

Early on, I learned some things that made my new job more difficult.

Initially, I was unaware of Charlie Badewicz's depth of displeasure with my appointment at TRE, although I could understand his disappointment at not getting the job. Remember, he had been "acting" after Dick's departure. Charlie had a good reputation as an engineer, but insisted on everything being done "his way." Working with or for an autocrat was not popular with the engineering community or anyone else in the company's management. On the surface, he was friendly and accommodating to me. But apparently, he thought the company had made a terrible mistake in hiring me. He led a cabal against my leadership, actively working to unseat me.

He was joined in this endeavor by two strong-willed senior executives of TRA: Roy Fields, former TRA Vice President of Finance, and Bill Wiley, the Vice President of Manufacturing, who was also responsible for that function here at TRE. They spoke openly against my leadership to management and employees in both companies. At some point, Charlie felt strong enough to carry his argument to Barry Shillito, the President of TRA. Barry was also my nominal boss, since TRE was a division of TRA.

Charlie had many skills, but political intrigue wasn't one of them. Barry wasn't born yesterday, and certainly knew that George Roberts (especially) and Bill Rutherford, were behind my appointment. Barry would be loath to interfere with that chain of command, and certainly wouldn't do so on behalf of a complaining, "passed over" VP. Nothing changed after all this, but it certainly didn't make my job any easier or more pleasant. It came at a time when we all needed to pull together.

A PHONE CALL FROM THE PAST

I noted earlier that I was good friends with Brigadier General Mike Dunn, the vice-president's military attache'. Roughly a year after leaving the White House, I received a call from Mike. He said, "Hudson, you have to come to Washington as soon as possible. Something big is In the wind." I said, "Hey, Mike, I'm In a new job, I can't just go running off to Washington." He said, "Bring Joan, I'll meet you in the dining room of the Madison Hotel. Just give me the date and time."

In spite of our misgivings, Joan and I went, and met Mike at the restaurant. He wasted no time telling us that President Nixon would resign, and Vice President Agnew would be the next president! Watergate evidence was building up, and it was very unlikely that the president would be able to continue in office... it was just a matter of time. We were stunned!

I asked Mike, "So, what does this have to do with me?" He said, "Hudson, the vice president wants you in his cabinet!" OMG! He went on to explain what was going on in the administration in more detail, and I had to agree, it all seemed to make sense. What a shocker! Joan and I returned to San Diego in something of a daze.

About a month later, the Baltimore Sun newspaper broke the story that the vice president, as Baltimore County Executive, and as Governor of Maryland, was accused of accepting bribes from contractors.

He resigned the vice presidency on October 10, 1973.

As Mike prophesized, the president did resign on August 9, 1974, but the newspaper expose' of the vice president, blew up his plans in spades!

The flow of events In those days was stunning...and what might have been, even more so!

DEVELOPING TALENT

I have always believed in looking into an organization, finding promising young talent, and bringing it out to develop and grow. I looked after these people, handed them challenging assignments, gave them room for trial and error, taught them to trust in their own skills and strengths, and supported their decisions. The product of this approach was a thriving pool of young men and women ready to step into bigger jobs and responsibilities as positions opened up and programs developed. Another life lesson.

MARS

I knew we had a talented team of engineers and manufacturing personnel at TRE who were dedicated to the task and willing to put in the effort to get the job done. We delivered the radars to support the launches. VIKING 1 launched on August 20, 1975, and landed on July 20, 1976. VIKING 2 launched on September 9, 1975, and landed on September 3, 1976.

It took the spacecraft 11 months to travel the 300 million miles to Mars, and when it got there, our altimeter and landing radar worked as advertised! It was the first mission to land a spacecraft safely on the surface of Mars and return images of the surface. It took photographs and collected scientific data on the Martian surface. TRE was justly proud.

The VIKING MISSION TO MARS was a major accomplishment!

**Illustration of the VIKING Spacecraft
on the surface of MARS**

While VIKING was successful, we had put everything into the effort. Once it was over the question was *what are we going to do next?* We had focused totally on VIKING, and found ourselves now woefully short of products. We had the old APN-182 Klystron (tube) powered Doppler that had been in production for some years, and was to be phased out. We also had the new, first solid-state Doppler Radar in development for the Navy, the APN-200. It had a small, planar array (flat) antenna in lieu of the large old "bathtub" transmit and receive antennas associated with the APN-182, but was not yet in production.

I was facing a really serious problem at TRE. Once VIKING shipped, revenue fell and manpower had to be adjusted accordingly, both direct and indirect. Our engineering headcount rapidly dropped below 100, and the chief engineer told me that we were losing core talent which would be very difficult to replace.

I met with my marketing director, Allen Osborne. I found he had no real plan put together for us other than the Navy order of APN-200's for their new S-3A aircraft, assuming of course, that it passed all the necessary testing. Clearly not enough to mean much at this point.

I asked about increasing sales of the 182 by approaching the Navy.

"The Navy won't talk to us, since we don't have a standalone product." He told me.

"What?"

"Well, we have the Doppler sensor, but without a Computer Display Unit (CDU), the radar doesn't contribute anything useable." He replied.

In other words, the crew needed position information (latitude-longitude) from the CDU to fly, and we could not provide it with just the radar. It also meant that we couldn't market or sell our equipment to the Navy customer directly, and had to rely on someone else to sell our equipment as part of their system. That was disappointing news indeed, and a "big hole in our quiver."

No question, we needed to design and develop our own CDU as quickly as possible. I couldn't imagine why it hadn't been done sooner, though I assumed the demands of the APOLLO Program (TRE had built the Landing Radar for the Lunar Excursion Module) had been similar to those of the VIKING Program. Working under pressure from the customer, government, and company management precluded anybody doing anything except trying to get an important job done on budget and on schedule.

Of course, the CDU would take time and cost money. Here was another problem.

APOLLO 17 Astronauts at TRE celebration (left to right, Me, Ron Evans, Gene Cernan, Jack Schmitt). The Lunar Excursion Module Landing Radar is in the foreground. This was the last APOLLO mission to land men on the Moon. 1972.

PACIFIC GROUP ORGANIZATION

Let me explain how the Pacific Group of Teledyne's companies operated. Bill Rutherford was the Pacific Group Executive. He was at TRA when Teledyne bought the company in 1969 for $128M. As noted earlier, Bill was a Stanford man, with a BS in Accounting. He was a man of few words, and had a dry sense of humor. Emphasis on dry. Companies usually saw him only at Profit Plan meetings, along with his staff.

He was assisted by three sub-group executives, who were each responsible for three or four group companies. My group executive was Roy Fields. He was responsible for Teledyne Ryan Aeronautical (TRA), Teledyne Ryan Electronics (TRE), and Teledyne AeroCal (a metal forming company in nearby San Marcos).

Roy was five or so years older than me, a San Diego State graduate with a degree in Accounting. That was his background and his interest. Following the VIKING mission, he was all over TRE, eager to make immediate headcount reductions consistent with the falling revenue.

While we understood the rationale, we were not happy to lose key skills at the very moment we needed them for new product development. Roy was interested in cash flow, and I was interested in a new product, without which there would be no cash flow! This did not play well with Roy. As you might expect, this led to some tense meetings between Roy and me. We managed to butt heads not only at TRE, but also at the weekly staff meeting held at TRA by President Barry Shillito, who technically presided over both the Ryan companies, but was also under Roy.

I think it's fair to say that Roy and I just didn't really like each other; it was a personality thing. He struck me as a negative, basically unhappy person. I understood that he had had a tough divorce, which may have contributed. All this said, however, he was my boss and I had to do my best to get along with him. So I did.

I was reminded of something my grandfather told me years earlier, when I had to do something I didn't want to do. "Sometimes you

just have to put on a tin beak and peck shit with the chickens!"
More life lessons.

CDU DEVELOPMENT

The good news was that by hook or crook and IR&D (Independent Research and Development), my technical people developed a computer display unit (CDU) under Bob Chapman's leadership. This was our ticket for getting into navigation "systems!"

I recall taking the new CDU to the corporate office for a Profit Plan meeting with Dr. Singleton. I set up the demo on the floor by an electrical outlet and keyed in some flight information so we could show him how the CDU worked. When I looked up, he was on his knees next to me to "check it all out!" He was very complimentary, and understood the signal importance of the CDU to our business. To wit, we now had a "navigation system," not just a subsystem sensor, and we could market it to the defense department and others ourselves. We had an important new product!

I made some management changes, including a new marketing director.

PERSONAL DEVELOPMENT

In 1974, I decided that it would be wise from a career standpoint to get an MBA degree. I settled on Pepperdine University in Malibu, California which was accessible and had an attractive program, the "Presidential Key Executive." The program was organized over 19 months for senior working executives.

It met three days a month, which wasn't too bad, but also required a thesis! Studying hours at home, coupled with age, taught me that I needed glasses if I wanted to avoid headaches. I got my first pair of "readers."

I signed up with the knowledge that I'd receive my degree in 1976, on the country's 200th birthday. What a way to celebrate! Teledyne paid the tuition and fees. It was a lot of work, but it expanded my horizons in many ways and I believe it was a good investment in "me." My thesis was on Systems Development and I received my MBA on schedule. Some of the faculty felt that the quality of my thesis should make me an "honors" graduate. The Dean, however, demurred because my thesis subject was not a "pure business" subject!

Meanwhile at home, we decided to put in a solar-heated 20' by 40' swimming pool. We all enjoyed it and I started a long-term practice of swimming laps, not just at home, but also on road trips. Our home was next to the 14th fairway of the Rancho Bernardo Golf Club, a wedge shot to the green. We joined the club, but a year or so later, we decided to change to another club. The Stoneridge Country Club had a much younger membership. Joan and Howard started golf lessons.

CANCER

Soon after we moved to Rancho Bernardo, Joan was diagnosed with breast cancer. She opted for a radical surgery and her breast was removed, followed by radiation. She was a fighter and despite how she felt, she continued her long walks in Rancho Bernardo.

Over the years, she would have this or that pop up, and it would be handled successfully by her Oncology team. One night, she woke me up saying, "I've done something bad to my leg." We discovered that the cancer had eaten through her femur, the largest bone in the body! Surgeons put a titanium bar in her leg to replace the bone. She returned home and, in time, returned to walking. Albeit with a slight limp.

While the boys were young, Joan would never travel with me. But, as they matured, we reached the point where she could join me. We traveled to the Paris Air Show, Belgium, Switzerland, Japan, Israel, Egypt and other places of interest which we both enjoyed. We also had Season Tickets to the Charger games (as many Ryan employees did) and we did serious "tailgating" at the stadium before the games with our friends and Ryan colleagues.

THE FUTURE

In the mid-70s, after the VIKING equipment shipped, my concern regarding a viable company product and the defense electronics market was considerable. I was worried, not only about the future of TRE, but also myself and my family.

For example, Joan and I had friends in Rancho Bernardo. They were 10 years or so older than us, and they had built a spectacular custom home on a hill overlooking the golf club and course. The three bedroom, two bath home was on a big lot and had a lovely yard, including a lap pool. Its main attraction was a huge family/great room, with beam ceiling and a massive fireplace of beautiful sandstone set flat so the edges showed. The house looked out over the golf course, amazing! I estimate it was 3500 sq. ft. or so.

They had decided to sell it and move to Del Mar and build a bigger house of the same design. It was on the market for $400,000. Joan wanted that house in the worst way. By selling our home we could swing the purchase, but I was concerned about the future. How could we commit to a new house under such circumstances? It was painful to tell her that I just didn't feel it was in our best interest to buy at that time. Joan was disappointed, but understanding. A year or so later, everything had settled down work-wise. Looking back, it would have been a great buy.

Timing is everything. A life lesson.

MOTHER EARTH

In 1975 I got to thinking about a back-up...sort of. Our home in North County was close to hills. I had noticed avocado groves in the area, which were planted on hillsides because of drainage issues. Citrus was also present, both oranges and lemons. After checking on tax effects, I found that citrus groves had to "be in production" before you could write anything off. That took a good five years or more! Avocado development expenses, on the other hand, could be written off as incurred.

Between the tax advantages and the going market price of avocados, I worked the numbers for the purchase of land and its attendant development for avocados. It wasn't as good as discovering oil, but I thought it was workable. I had enjoyed Botany classes at UCLA for my Life Science requirements, and thought it would be a worthwhile endeavor. Theoretically, it could add some income while providing a retirement home/ranch, a tax break, and direct access to fresh guacamole!

First, however, I took classes offered by the county of San Diego on the "cultural needs of avocados." I worked with a land broker named Gene Gillette. We found a suitable piece of property in the Highland Valley area near Starvation Mountain, NW of the city of Ramona. Purchased for $40,000, it was about only 20-25 minutes from our home.

I also bought a new 1976 four-wheel drive Ford F-150 with big tires. I equipped it with an eight-track tape deck and big speakers in the doors. At the grove we entertained ground squirrels, rattlesnakes, and condors with the likes of Janis Joplin, The Eagles, Fleetwood Mac, and Boston. It was fun and made the hard work more tenable. We also acquired a Honda three-wheeler for use around the property. The land had gentle slopes, decomposed granite (perfect) and faced southeast. The terrain was steep enough to avoid frost damage as well. There was no electric power or other services on-site.

GETTING STARTED

We had 23.3 acres to work with and hired a professional to layout the planting, drip irrigation system, fertilizer injection system, grove roads... and everything else! He put the trees on 20' centers and we planted 2,300. There was plenty of migrant labor available at $5.00/hr. and my high school and college Spanish was very useful!

At the time, avocado trees were in high demand. You had to order them and wait for delivery. In addition, you bought only from a reputable grower to avoid disasters such as "root rot" and other avocado diseases.

I was fortunate to get an order in to Bill Frey, a very reputable grower in the nearby city of Escondido. On advice from my land broker, I ordered and planted a mix of varieties. As I recall, about ½ Hass, 1/3 Bacon (especially on the low property), and the rest in Reeds, Santanas, and other varieties. I realized fairly quickly that I should have planted more Hass, since that was where the market was going. So I brought in an expert who "top worked" many of the Bacon variety. He grafted Hass onto the Bacon root stock and essentially changed them to the Hass variety. It was a good call.

Between my family, my job, the MBA program, and the grove I was plenty busy! I was at the grove around 5:30 every morning to check the irrigation system, inject fertilizer if required and otherwise make sure all was in order. Walking the grove in my office attire, I was the best dressed "Grover" in the county! I arrived at the office by 8:00 a.m. and usually stayed until 6:00. Joan always griped that "I was the last man home on the street!"

COMMITMENT

Graduate school was, of course, scheduled. I spent weekends and vacations with the avocado trees. There was always work to be done! Frequently, coyotes would chew the plastic drip lines for water, and if you didn't pay attention you could lose trees quickly. Avocado trees are very shallow rooted and thirsty. The boys earned extra money helping me with spraying weed oil, cutting weeds, spreading straw etc. It was very hot in the summer.

We carried on the truck a large container of iced tea mixed with lemonade, before I knew what an "Arnold Palmer" was. The heat was particularly hard on Paul with his heart condition, so he wasn't there much during hot spells. Howard was a big help to me over the years there. On occasion, at the end of the day, we would pop a few cold beers sitting on the tailgate of the truck. A just reward for a hard day!

ANTI SHIP MISSILE DEFENSE RADAR

In the Tonkin Gulf, during the Vietnam War, there was an incident wherein a U.S. ship, the USS Sterrettt (CG-31) was attacked by a "sea skimming" (low flying) anti-ship missile fired from a North Vietnamese shore battery. It was believed to be a Russian STYX Missile, which was fast, and had a very low radar cross section (RCS). Since the Sterrett's surface radar could not detect it, the ship didn't know It was under attack, and so made no response. The Navy was shocked by this new threat.

The Navy's Bureau of Ships (BuShips) issued an RFP (request for proposal) and sent representatives to TRE (among other companies), to discuss an Emergency Fast Reaction program to counter this significant threat. The Navy wanted a radar system to test in nine weeks!

TRE is an airborne navigation house, but after reviewing the RFP, the technical staff developed a novel solution to the threat. They believed that we should utilize as much of the existing ship's Surface Search Radar as possible, but design a system which would utilize "Doppler Shift" technology. In the new system, the radar would be turned "on its side" as opposed to pointing toward the Earth as in an airborne system. Essentially, it would provide a solution to the threat by identifying a target by its velocity (see discussion at the beginning of this chapter).

The system we designed was much more than a "Doppler Radar." A key part of it, however, was incorporating the "Doppler Shift." The

SPS-10 Surface Radar on the Sterrett was not capable of detecting the incoming missile because it was flying low over the water and couldn't be "seen" due to the "clutter" (echoes/return on a radar screen that do not come from the target…in this case, a return caused by slow moving waves). An incoming missile traveling at 200 mph or more, would be easily differentiated from wave caused clutter. It would then be "filtered" out by the computer, and reported accordingly.

Our approach included four basic parts:

1) We designed an antenna that was long horizontally so it produced a beam that looked like a fan. Narrow left to right, but very wide in the vertical axis. Any object in the way would reflect a return signal.

2) If we received a return signal, we would know its direction by the positon of the antenna.

3) We would know if it were coming toward us (an up Doppler shift), or away from us (a down Doppler shift).

4) And, we would know how far away from us it was by the time it took a signal to return.

A computer would keep track of these targets from radar "scan to scan" (or revolution), which would be every four seconds. The computer would read the "Doppler shift" so it could discriminate/pick up targets by virtue of their velocity and thus determine if they were a threat.

We tested the new system by taking it to the coast at Torrey Pines Park, and setting it up on the cliff. Our test vehicle was a Dodge

Econoline van, equipped with a ship's SPS-10 Antenna mounted on the roof, and our radar electronics inside. We then asked the Navy at the Miramar Naval Air Station, to fly A-4 Skyhawk Aircraft to sea at a range greater than 50 miles. The aircraft would then turn inbound toward Torrey Pines at 50 feet "off the deck," simulating an incoming missile. The A-4's were used because they had a one square meter RCS, the equivalent of the Russian STYX Missile... which was classified at the time.

A "GO" FOR SHIP TESTING

The testing proved that we could detect incoming targets, and the Navy told us to proceed with ship based testing at Pearl Harbor. We were required to build nine systems...and we had to do it in nine weeks or less! The team virtually slept in the plant to get it done...but they did!

Communications went quiet while the Navy tested the various systems at sea. There were some big surprises when the results came in.

We learned that Westinghouse, our competitor and the Navy's historic surface radar supplier, could not get their radar equipment in the ship's radar room! It required an eight-foot cubed container, and had to be strapped down to the deck. Westinghouse had cobbled together a system using parts from various shipboard radars they manufactured. They were vacum tube intensive, and therefore, bulky. Our system was mostly solid state, designed to fit into the space allotted by the RFP for the radar. Furthermore, the Westinghouse equipment required air conditioning due to vacum tubes; the TRE system did not. During the six-week sea trials, TRE tracked every single target and detected every single incoming missile simulation! Westinghouse only got its equipment active for three days out of the six week trials, and never successfully tracked an incoming missile.

YOU CAN'T BE SERIOUS!

Westinghouse' manifold problems, however, were judged "correctible" by the Navy and they were awarded the contract. In my view, the decision reflected serious problems.

As noted earlier, the Navy hated adding weight to the mast such as with an additional antenna, which Westinghouse was planning to do. Our team came up with the great solution of using the existing SPS-10 Surface Radar. We duplexed, meaning that both frequencies (the one from our ASMDR and the SPS-10's) could be transmitted simultaneously and not interfere with one another. Every revolution of the antenna was used by both radars with no added top side weight or complexity!

The second identifiable issue was that Westinghouse was the incumbent Navy surface radar supplier. That meant there were many Navy bureaucrats and fleet officers as well closely tied into the company by virtue of purchasing and supporting their systems over a period of years. This was buttressed by the Westinghouse Washington, D.C. office which performed the usual "wining and dining" of its Navy customers.

Keeping customers happy is fine, but in times of crisis, the Navy should be "All hands on deck." When I went to Washington and called on the responsible Navy Program Office, I asked how they came to their decision. I was told "When the Navy buys a surface radar for the fleet, it's a Westinghouse Radar," period!

The third issue was that this procurement was a Fast Reaction Program brought on by a sudden and serious threat to the fleet. The usual, relatively slow, regular procurement process was not involved. Somehow, the Navy decision makers found Westinghouse' shortcomings "correctible," which in my opinion was really a stretch!

Correctible under what sort of time frame? Given the significant threat, It seemed irresponsible to take an unknown number of months fixing the many Westinghouse problems. What about the vulnerability of our ships In the meantime...?

FINALLY

A fourth point is that the Navy bureaucracy went out of its way to avoid a new, mostly solid state addition to the fleet that was capable of handling incoming threats from the sea. Our system was smaller, dimensionally correct, lighter, needed no air conditioning and added no top side weight. I can't begin to calculate how much better our "mean time between failure" (MTBF) rate would be compared to their vacuum tube technology system. Finally, the TRE system would be significantly cheaper. But, the main point is, if time was as critical as the Navy professed, what were they thinking selecting Westinghouse? Would the men at risk on our fighting ships have made the same decision?

In any case, fate intervened. The Paris Peace Accords were signed and the war ended, as did the ASMDR Program.

There were a number of key engineers on our technical team. But Charles Sparks, the Project Engineer, and Gene Dotson, the Lead Microwave Engineer, were the drivers. In many ways these men represented the creativity and teamwork that led TRE to many of its wins over the following years.

AN AIR FORCE OPPORTUNITY

In early 1976, the company was awarded a competitive development contract by the U.S. Air Force's Aeronautical Systems Division (ASD) at Wright Patterson Air Force Base in Dayton, Ohio. It was a significant opportunity for us with a new customer, the U.S. Air Force! The contract called for the design and manufacture of a Doppler Radar Navigation System (DRNS) which would replace existing, outdated systems in the B-52G and H series bombers, and the KC-135 inflight re-fueling aircraft. Both aircraft and radar had been given new, unique and stringent requirements.

The new radar system was not only required to meet more difficult velocity, accuracy, and altitude objectives. It also needed to be nuclear hardened against thermo-nuclear conditions. Competitors were required to design and test six prototype radar systems and deliver them to ASD, which would perform extensive flight, environmental, reliability, and nuclear hardness testing.

The radar also had to meet the very stiff reliability requirement of 1000 hours MTBF (mean time between failures), guaranteed by the contractor. This was an unheard of requirement at that time! It does, however, reflect the tremendous improvement in electronics reliability brought about by the new solid state technology.

Our design approach utilized a new concept that incorporated several risky, but innovative ideas. If they worked, they would provide exceptional performance. These new ideas were called Automatic Terrain Bias, a capability that would provide better accuracy performance than previous designs. At the same time, the use of a new Planar Array Antenna would improve high altitude performance.

The B-52 and KC-135 were key aircraft in the USAF Strategic Air Command (SAC) fleet. Portions of the fleet and crews were kept on 24/7 emergency alert. Once a War Order was issued, SAC was required to launch its aircraft within 15 to 25 minutes. Aircraft began moving toward take-off positions within minutes of the alert notification. The rapid movement of the aircraft preparing for take-off did not allow sufficient time for the onboard Inertial Navigation System (INS) to properly calibrate itself.

I PLUS I = 3!

Under normal circumstances, the INS would require 25 to 30 minutes of static warmup time to properly align its gyros. Each INS had three gyros, one for each axis in space (pitch, roll, and yaw). The INS functions on the principle that its very sensitive gyros, when fully "spun-up" would North-seek by sensing the earth's rotation, which caused these extremely sensitive gyros to precess[2] in the direction of the North Pole, hence its ability to find direction.

The INS utilized accelerometers to determine velocity. The DRNS used an entirely different principle to sense velocity. As noted earlier, the radar creates four very narrow beams of microwave energy pointed towards the earth's surface. The "shift" in the reflected signal's frequency is directly proportional to the aircraft's velocity. When that is combined with information from the aircraft's heading reference system, the crew could navigate the aircraft.

---

2   Precession: The movement of the axis or rotation of a spinning body around another axis outside the body, and at an angle to it. An effect generated by a spinning gyro.

The INS and DRNS had *different* but *complementary* qualities. When combined they provided a superior, *self-contained* navigation system. This means they were not dependent on anything outside the aircraft. The velocity provided by the Doppler radar was instantly available upon movement of the aircraft, and could be used by the crew to navigate while the INS gyros were being spun up. A unique mathematical model, Kalman Filter, was installed as a software program in the aircraft's navigation computer. The computer then made continuous decisions regarding which system provided the best navigation solution. It was known as a "bounded error" system. We delivered our six prototype radars for Air Force testing and hoped for the best.

A PRESIDENCY

One day I received a call from Dr. Roberts about the Teledyne Hastings Raydist Company, in Hampton Roads, Virginia. Its president and founder, Charlie Hastings, had passed away. George said they were looking for a new president. He suggested I go and visit to determine any interest I might have.

I traveled to Charlotte and met the group executive, Herb Barnard. The company was small, approximately five million dollars in revenue, but extremely profitable. Its business was very precise measurement used in offshore positioning of ships involved in oceanographic and scientific work, oil platforms, and minesweeping for the defense department. The "Raydist" system used a network of beacons for its precise positioning.

It was very warm and humid in Hampton Roads, and I wondered about the possible effect on Paul's health. When I got home, I called his cardiologist. He said that Paul could take the heat, or the humidity. Not both. While I appreciated the opportunity from Teledyne, I said, "No thanks."

A significant customer of ours was the Iranian Navy (IN). Under Foreign Military Sales Legislation (FMS) they purchased a number of SH-3 Helicopters from the United States. As noted earlier, the SH-3 carried our APN-182 Radar,

I made several trips to Iran, and came to know the Commander of the Iranian Navy's Helicopter Wing, Admiral Ardalan. These were halcyon days for the Shah, he bought a great deal of military aircraft and hardware from the U.S., including Bell Helicopters. I will get to them later.

I was aware that we had sold the Iranians a number of spares, especially Klystron Tube power supplies...way more than what would be considered normal given their number of helicopter squadrons. We were happy to sell them all the spares they wanted, as that business carried a very nice profit margin.

One afternoon I received a phone call from the Admiral...from Teheran nonetheless! He told me that they were desperate for power supplies, and would I be so kind as to bring them as many as possible immediately, and, oh, by the way, he wanted to discuss a new order for our radars!

"You should have plenty of power supplies in stock." I said.

He said, "I know we do, but we can't find them."

A long story short, I agreed to bring as many as I could.

LAND OF AGHA KAHN

As I flew over the harbor on my approach to the Teheran (Meherab) Airport in Iran, looking out the window, I was amazed by the number of ships clogged up in the harbor and backed up way out to sea! No wonder they couldn't find what they needed. So much for sound logistics support!

My trip itself was noteworthy... I had flown from LAX to Munich non-stop, and caught a Lufthansa 707 (first class, when it was really First Class!) non-stop to Teheran. I was sitting very comfortably in my seat when a stewardess brought me a large frozen glass, filling it to the brim with Russian Vodka. Another stewardess brought me a whole can of beluga caviar, complete with all the condiments. It had to be at least eight ounces!

Well, there I was, "pigging out" on the vodka and caviar when a steward rolled down the aisle with, honest to God, a whole roasted pig. It even had an apple in its mouth! Unbelievable, I loved it! Today, there would certainly be no pork served going into Iran!

One other comment on Iran, was their deference to royalty. It happened to a number of Teledyne travelers, not just me. We had reservations at a first class hotel, a necessity. Our reservation was for three nights. However, at the end of the first day we came back to the hotel and found our luggage piled up in the hallway, with whatever was in the closet on top of it all! We went down to the desk to find out what was going on. They simply replied that Sheik Omar (or whoever) had come into town, and taken the whole floor over! Not even a "Sorry" for our trouble.

Teledyne solved this problem. The company bought a two-story villa, installed a Teledyne Manager and his wife on the first floor, and converted the second floor into five bedrooms with a large shower/bathroom in the middle. The first manager was the infamous "Doc Sloan" from TRA and the Vietnam days. We had a great time!

AN ARMY OPPORTUNITY

The U.S. Army came out with an RFP (request for proposal) for a lightweight Doppler Radar Navigation System, (LDNS). This would not only be our first bid as a "systems" house, but the Army was the largest helicopter market in the Department of Defense (DoD). Helicopters were prime users of Doppler Radar Navigation. The Army represented the largest quantity but also the lowest average price. We considered it a must win. Our competition was Singer-Kearfott, a major Doppler Systems company known for low prices.

The Army Program Manager for LDNS was Lt. Col. Roy White, located at Fort Monmouth, New Jersey. Our team worked hard on Col. White both at our plant and in New Jersey. He was a very likeable man, but we had no real insight into his personal or official opinions. As you would expect, Singer was also courting him.

Charlie Badewicz was our program manager for the LDNS proposal. He was in charge of the key proposal effort for my company. Once I knew he'd gone around me to meet with Barry, and continued to undermine my leadership, I could not keep the man. I arranged his transfer to another Teledyne Company, which he later left for another opportunity. I am reminded of a classic saying from my mother that describes the situation with Charlie: "It's better to have an empty house than a bad tenant." I appointed Chuck Sparks (Sparky) the new LDNS Program Manager. He did everything one could do (legally) to assure a win.

We put together the very best technical and cost proposal we could. I should add here, that TRE did not have the pricing function. That was done by Jim Webb at TRA, and under Roy's watchful eye. I had no input re what we bid price-wise.

RATTLERS AND RODENTS

Meanwhile, back at the grove, we battled rattle snakes and gophers on a daily basis. The snakes came out to sun themselves. They were very hard to see against the decomposed granite and natural landscape. I carried a .22 caliber rifle in a rack in the truck, but trying to kill a rattler with it was a joke…something I learned quickly. I bought a .38 caliber frame pistol with a .22 caliber barrel, and loaded it with bird shot ammo.

All you had to do was point it in the general direction of the snake and pull the trigger to "perforate" the snake with lots of shot. I always carried the pistol in a holster on my hip. Fortunately, no one was ever bitten. Or shot!

Gophers in a commercial grove are anathema! They're a real enemy, and can do incredible damage to tree roots in short order. I was a good customer of the Grangetto's Farm Supply Company in Escondido where I bought nitrogen fertilizer, implements, and other supplies for the grove. They advised me to try a particular device in my fight against gophers.

At the grove, surrounded by Haas Avocado trees.

It was shaped like a long "tee," perhaps 3 feet long. On the top was a container for poisoned grain and raisins (smelled great) with a crank and a hollow tube, which ran down to a point where there was a hole. When you saw fresh dirt from a gopher, you'd prod around with the point of the device to find the tunnel. Once you found the entrance, you simply turned the crank one or two rotations to release the poison grain into the tunnel. You removed the device and placed a rock over the hole. Presto! No more gopher.

RULE # I

Rule #1 at the grove was to never leave an active gopher site without dealing with it. As you might expect, virtually every time we were leaving for the day we would find a site that needed fixing! I am happy to tell you that in all the years we had the grove we didn't lose one single tree to gophers!

The grove was doing great, and we joined the Calavo cooperative. We were picking a fair amount of fruit, which was rewarding, not just due to the young age of the trees, but financially as well. The Hass avocado (dark, pebbly skin) would bring $.90 to $1.00 a pound, while the "greens" (Bacons etc.) brought $.75 to $.85 a pound. The "top work" paid off! Calavo required that "before" you picked, you had to bring in three avocados of the variety you were going to pick for testing.

The avocados had to meet their standard of at least eight percent oil content. That's what gives them their flavor. If you passed inspection, you were free to pick (obviously) subject to market price fluctuations of avocados.

Joan and I would pick up two large metal bins at Calavo for the fruit. Each bin held about 1000 pounds. So, when we went to "market" (Calavo), we brought in two bins, or about one ton of avocados in the bed of the pick-up truck.

Picking was a family affair, and while we had help, it was a satisfying effort. Joan and I always went together to deliver the fruit.

LAND OF THE RISING SUN

The Japanese Maritime Defense Force (JMDF) purchased FMS (Foreign Military Sale) Sikorsky SH-3 Helicopters, which they primarily used for anti-submarine warfare (ASW). The governments of the United States and Japan had an arrangement whereby if the

JMDF procured a U.S. aircraft, certain subsystems would be licensed to Japanese companies to manufacture.

We supplied the APN-182 Doppler Radar for the SH-3, and that was one of the subsystems on the list to license. The JMDF selected the Mitsubishi Electric Company (MELCO), and it chose the Yamada Company to represent it in the negotiations with us for our radar as their agent. The Yamada representatives that came to San Diego to negotiate the license were Ohtsu-san, Miyazaki-san and an engineer whose name I don't remember.

Navy Lt. Jeff Wallin and I prior to a flight in the SH-3 Helicopter to demonstrate the APN-182's Doppler Navigation System.

The negotiations were lengthy and the conference room was thick with cigarette smoke from the Japanese, all of whom smoked. Perhaps it wouldn't have been a big deal under ordinary conditions, but I had just quit smoking days before they arrived, and it was killing me! I persevered, however. I never smoked again after 30 some years as a confirmed smoker. We reached an agreement and had an excellent and profitable relationship with Yamada for many years. More on this later.

SORRY NEWS

One day, Joan drove up to the grove. She rarely came up unless she was bringing lunch or joining us for a beer. That day she brought neither. She told me that we had been notified by the Army that Singer-Kearfott had won the LDNS contract! To say I was devastated would be an understatement, "crushed" would be more appropriate. It was so disappointing.

In high school, I had frequented an auto parts store with a prominent sign posted by the cash register: "We have no quarrel with those who sell for less, they know what they're stuff is worth!"

I felt for the team that had worked so hard and for so long on the proposal, and for our company that needed this contract in the worst way. I felt sorry for myself too, as the leader. It was disappointing to come up short on a "must win" program. We knew we had technical advantages, but with the Army, cost was king, and Singer had the lowest price. Life may not be fair, but you have to play the cards you're dealt. The LDNS loss was painful, but we learned from the experience. What's next? A life lesson.

A NAVY OPPORTUNITY

The next opportunity for us was from the U.S. Navy. They put out an RFP for a program called "LAMPS," Light Attack Multi-Purpose System, a Doppler Navigation System for the new SH-60B Helicopter. Bill McClure was our program manager. The Navy was an old and valued customer of ours. Our working relationship went back years, all the way to the APN-130, and more recently with the APN-182, which was currently in the fleet.

The APN-182 was made up of the radar, power supply, and two large antennas, plus several connecting cables. Our contender for the LAMPS program was our new APN-217. This radar contained everything in "one box." This was a huge improvement, not to mention a planar array antenna and lighter weight, an important component in the competition.

The Systems Integrator for LAMPS was the Federal Systems Division of IBM, a customer of ours located in Armonk, New York. My new Director of Marketing, Peter Murphy and I spent a lot of time working on Dell Babb, the IBM Program Manager, and the other team members. We did all the usual things during the process: attending appropriate conventions and shows, calling on the customer and the fleet, etc.

While the quantities were less than the Army's LDNS, the radars were more expensive, driven by the technical requirements of navigating over water, a difficult surface for radar. We worked really hard on the proposal.

Once again, Singer-Kearfott was the major competition…but this time around, we won! I called for an "all hands" party at a local restaurant, Kobe Misono, to celebrate our contract. We received about $12M in non-recurring engineering and tooling, for three prototype test units. There would be a lot of follow-on business, not only for the SH-60B helicopters, but MH-53E and others!

SOME RECOGNITION

In 1975 I was awarded the Silver Knight of Management by the National Management Association, upon the recommendation of the Ryan Electronics Company's management club.

I felt it was time to do something for our employees. We scheduled an "open house," with tours of the offices and factory (with our new three axis machine tool) and a BBQ. There's a lot to be gained from hot dogs, drinks, and a positive atmosphere! One thing I learned from this experience was that when you wanted the factory to be "clean", schedule a family event! Works great! Another life lesson.

The employees and their families enjoyed the day. My folks drove down from Laguna Beach to join the fun and see the plant for the first time. Sometime during the day, I walked into my office and my mom was sitting on the couch...smoking! "Mom," I said, "you can't smoke in the plant, it's against the law!"

She simply said, "Not a problem, my son runs the place!"

A LESSON IN "INTERIOR DESIGN"

The factory area at TRE had large "tilt up" concrete walls, a good 20' high, and painted a light tan. The concrete wall separating the factory area from the offices provided the main corridor across the building and was about 150' long. It served as the main thorough-fare for both employees and customers. In a word, it was "dull." I remember at the Autonetics facility the interior walls were painted a weak pea green. Just awful!

I was driving to work one day, listening to the radio. San Diego State University (SDSU) ran a commercial encouraging San Diegans to hire SDSU art students for creative work at the home or office. I jotted down the number. When I got to the office, I asked Sharon to get someone on the line so I could talk to them about a job. I had some ideas about sprucing up the interior of the plant. I told the person on the phone that I wanted not only a creative artist, but one with vision, who could/would paint on a vertical cement wall, using our products and the aircraft or helicopters in which they flew. I definitely wanted a "free thinker."

SDSU sent out a young man named Don Lebow for me to interview. He brought his rather impressive portfolio with him. I showed him our products and aircraft and some thoughts of things that might surround them. I took him onto the factory floor, and showed him the wall. Don said, "Man, this has scale." I hired him and set him loose.

Don was a terrific young artist who worked for months painting spectacular, innovative, and informative space and defense scenes on the wall. Employees and customers alike loved it! More on him later.

Around this time, TRE was approached by LITEF, the West German Division of Litton Industries, located in Frieburg. The general man-ager was Robert Hopman. They were interested in a radar for a special application in a new German aircraft, the ALPHA Jet. They wanted a license deal. As usual, the negotiations dragged on a bit, but we finally worked it out after each of us made several trips back and forth. LITEF ordered 20 radars which were designed around the LDNS Radar. This new radar was called the APN-220. It was encouraging to have another product, a new foreign customer, and a nice sale as well.

The Moroccan Air Force also purchased ALPHA Jets from West Germany. Gene Dotson, one of our top engineers, and I went there and called on the Air Force in Rabat. Their mission was different than the Luftwaffe, so no luck with the APN-220 in Morocco. Still a fascinating trip!

LAND OF THE PLUM BLOSSOMS

In early 1972, President Nixon broke a 25 year American separation from the Peoples Republic of China (PRC) by traveling there for substantive discussions. A year or so later, we received an inquiry from the China National Aero-technology Import-Export Corporation (CATIC), the PRC's tech center. They were interested in our APN-220 for their three new Cessna Citation II Aircraft, plus a spare. We exchanged correspondence which resulted in my flying to Beijing to meet with CATIC representatives in February.

I was met at the airport and taken to my hotel in a long, black Russian Zil limousine. My first impression of the city was the thick blanket of brown smog, presumably from the coal furnaces that provided heat to the city. The passenger windows were covered by a white lace "doily" that permitted you to see out, but prevented others from seeing In.

When we approached the hotel, which was located on Tiananmen Square, my second Impression was the square. It was huge, and, literally packed with people walking and riding black bicycles in every direction! There were no cars, none!

When the driver pulled into our hotel area, he just "pushed" in on the crowd of people with the limo without stopping. We really got dirty looks, and with good reason. I was glad they couldn't see me!

A DIFFERENT SORT OF HOTEL

The hotel, of course, was government run. I was shown to my one room plus bath by my "floor house boy." It was very basic, but included a phone and a big colorful thermos for making tea. Every time I left and locked my door, it was always wide open upon my return! One day, upon returning, I wanted to make some tea and complain about how cold the room was. But, the house boy had not refilled the hot water in my thermos. I walked down the hall where he had a desk. He wasn't there, but there were several curtain covered doorways behind the desk, so I poked my head in to see if he was there. He wasn't, so I looked in the next room. It was a narrow room with a bench running down the middle. On the walls on both sides of the bench were sets of earphones. OMG! My room was bugged! I closed the curtain and quickly went back to my room… undetected. My discovery was unnerving to say the least. I was certainly careful what I said on the telephone as well.

The next morning, the Zil limousine picked me up and took me to the CATIC Offices, again, driving through the pedestrians and bicycle riders as if they weren't there. I was introduced to Mr. Fu, the head of their negotiating team. He was a pleasant looking man, perhaps in his forties with a crew cut. He wore a well-tailored, black, Mandarin style suit. Mr. Fu was all of 4'10" tall, maximum!

We gathered in a conference room. I should mention that there was no heat in the building. When we spoke, you could see our breath. I noted that all the CATIC engineers wore a number of long sleeve sweaters. After a few days of meeting, I also noticed that their sweater patterns never changed, meaning that they hadn't changed clothes. The conference room had a decided personal aroma, mixed with serious garlic.

The CATIC engineers were convinced that the APN-220 would be acceptable, so the meeting turned into a negotiation. My interest was to open the Chinese Market for our products. They had plenty of aircraft and helicopters that could/should be using our equipment, if I could get our "nose under the tent" with the Citation II's. The CATIC people had not said anything directly, but it appeared to me that they "might" be interested in a license deal. We settled on $85,000/radar which covered my cost plus a modest profit.

To celebrate, the Chinese invited me to a real Peking Duck Dinner. Mr. Fu, the host, personally carved the duck breast, and put the slices carefully on my plate. It was a delightful evening in every way.

THE YANGTZE RIVER

Mr. Fu asked me what I would like to see in China. I told him I always wanted to see the Yangtze River. The next day, along with several engineers, we flew privately from Beijing to Shanghai, where we met a ship on the Huangpu River, just across from Pudong. Pudong was just a marsh in those days. Today it is a metropolis! We went down the river to the Yangtze and spent several hours cruising on its broad expanse. A thoroughly interesting day.

A comment on the food. I always liked Chinese food…but, of course that means American-Chinese food. In China, I lived on rice, bean sprouts, "thousand-year old eggs" (they were black) and their version of chicken soup. I carefully avoided the chicken beaks and feet that were in the soup, and concentrated on white meat, greens and dumplings.

Several months later, I returned to Beijing to check on the installations in their Citations, and see how the navigation systems were operating. In addition, I wanted to touch base regarding follow-on business, license possibilities etc. The three installs looked fine, and CATIC was happy with their performance. I looked around the hangar and asked where the spare radar was.

There was much "shoe shuffling" and coughing, but no answers. Finally, I posited that the radar must be at a university laboratory being "reverse engineered." That was clearly it, as their faces turned pink.

"Look," I said, "the hardest part of manufacturing the radar is the Impatt Diode in a tuned cavity that rings at 13.3 GHZ. If you can build such a transmitter at a decent price, I will buy all you can make." I never heard a peep from them, and nothing more about a license either.

NOTHING BEATS WINNING!

The U.S. Air Forces Common Doppler development had run for almost three years, 1976 to 1979. As mentioned earlier, TRE's design approach resulted in a superior system, so long as our new ideas "panned out." They did, and we won the competition! This was a huge win! ASD awarded us a production contract in 1979, with options, for up to 1,000 systems! Yes, we had another "all-hands" party!

Over the following years, more than 1,500 systems were delivered to the USAF. Variations of the original design were developed for the B1-B, FB-111 and AWACS aircraft. Our system was installed in 300 B-52's and 900 KC-135's. Wow! I happened to notice that the better our numbers were, the less I heard from my Group Executive…. hmmm!

A NEW COMPANY

On May 12, 1980, Roy came into my office and told me that Teledyne was separating Teledyne Ryan Electronics from Teledyne Ryan Aeronautical, and making Electronics a full-fledged Teledyne Inc. company! I was named as the new president. What a wonderful surprise!

It had taken eight years to get the company up and going, but we had done it. It was a very personal and rewarding moment for me. We had grown from some $7M in revenue to over $50M with positive cash flow, solid income, not to mention a growing backlog and headcount. Oh yes, you can bet we had another "all-hands" party!

I had always resented having another company in our building. With our expanded business base, I was delighted to reclaim the other 150,000 sq. ft. from the Digital Development Corporation. We did a modernization of the lobby area, and installed attractive TELEDYNE RYAN ELECTRONICS signage on the front of the building.

We completely re-did the front yard facing Balboa Avenue, removing the ugly and overgrown shrubs to install new plants, trees, grass and an irrigation system. Oh, and we put in a big flag pole as well. My company now looked as successful as it was, and I was very proud of it.

STANFORD

Bill Rutherford, a Stanford man, suggested through Roy that I attend the Stanford Executive Program (SEP). It was a three week, on-campus intense program that had built a strong reputation over the years. It would have been great to go, especially to such a world-renowned university like Stanford. I don't recall with clarity exactly why I cancelled out of the SEP, but I think it was because TRE had just been made a separate Teledyne Company. I felt there were important things to do, such as organization, that were necessary to launch the new company.

Bill (Roy) asked me again the next year to attend, and again, I declined. Frankly, I don't remember why. Since the reservation is non-cancellable, Bill sent Roy in my place.

Looking back, I see that I was too taken with my importance to TRE. I didn't dare to be gone for three weeks, no matter the purpose. That was poor judgement on my part, and I own it. This is another lesson of note. By the way, I did do the Executive Program at the Anderson School at UCLA in the early 1990s.

SOMETHING POSITIVE

I was out on the factory floor one day and overheard a supervisor criticizing an assembly worker for some malfeasance or other. When I returned to my office, I got to thinking about the negativity of criticism. Yes, of course people need to be corrected or the company or product won't be as good as it could and should be. But what about the other side of the coin, the side where a person is doing good work?

Where is the acclamation for a job well done? When do we applaud improvement, or lending someone a hand on the line? That person will get no support or encouragement for doing well other than his or her own feelings of satisfaction. I went home that night and asked Joan if she would help me put together a small reward to recognize a job done well, or done better…or even for a random act of kindness. We cut small squares of muslin, and then put in a handful of M &M's, brought the corners together, and tied it with a ribbon. We prepared about 30.

The next morning was my weekly staff meeting and the leadership was there. I explained that I wanted to try out something new, and it was called a "TREAT," a Teledyne Ryan Electronics Achievement Token. I wanted factory supervision (this was designed for factory workers primarily) to look for people "doing something right," or going above and beyond. Then, I wanted the supervisor to write a brief note telling the worker what he or she had done to merit this award, sign it, and put it under a TREAT bag on their workstation. Well, the factory manager was already making faces and squirming in his seat with obvious discomfort.

Bob Serrano was my factory manager. I told him I wanted him to specifically brief his supervisors on this program, period. I also wanted a weekly report from him advising how many had been awarded, to whom, and for what reason. Bob got a lot of TREATs from me to give! If anyone along the "front row" saw something that warranted one, Sharon would give it to him as well.

I think the program served its purpose. We probably ran it for two or three weeks, and I even got some notes of appreciation from some of the workers. It was interpreted by them as recognition for doing something well. I believed anything you could do to increase motivation, pride, or positive attitudes in your workforce contributed to workplace cohesion and spirit. That fed into higher productivity, better quality, and so on.

In 1984, the San Diego Union newspaper ran an article on TRE that said, among other things, "Drake…boosted sales at Ryan Electronics an average of 20% a year during his 12 years there. Industry observers say he also achieved a remarkably low professional employee turnover record, while instilling new product quality standards and improved morale." Retaining key employees is job one, another life lesson.

GIVING BACK

After Paul's successful heart surgery in D.C., I felt that I owed a personal debt to children's hospitals. I got in touch with Blair Sadler, the CEO of our local Children's Hospital and Health Center. I served on its board of trustees for six years, and was Chairman of the hospital's research corporation. It was a wonderfully fulfilling time. The boys were both involved in little league baseball, and I made every effort to be there for their games. I coached Paul's team. We vacationed several years at the La Jolla Beach and Tennis Club, and another year at the Palmilla Resort in Baja. Memorable times.

In the 1980's, I was active in the community. I served on the University of California-San Diego's Board of Governors, San Diego State's Board of Advisors, the Greater San Diego Chamber of Commerce Board, and as division director of the United Way Campaign.

I mentioned Bell Helicopter in Iran earlier. With all due respect to Bell, their representatives in-country at that time were sorely lacking in courtesy and good taste. Classic "ugly American." They all wore a type of uniform: bright red sport coat, tan slacks, cowboy boots, and a Stetson. One thing they all shared was an attitude. They were loud, boisterous and an embarrassment in my opinion. The locals clearly did not appreciate them.

PERSIAN CARPETS

During my trips to Iran, I had the opportunity to visit many places such as Isfahan, Shiraz, Azerbaijan, the Alborz Mountains and other beautiful places in the country. On the other hand, when I visited Isfahan, a major producer of Persian carpets, I visited a local workshop. While everyone admires the beauty and workmanship of these carpets, I was not prepared for the conditions under which they were made.

It was wintertime, and the workshop was damp and cold. There was no heat. A large loom was set up in the middle of the room. Sitting cross-legged on wooden planks in front of the loom were eight of so very young children, hand weaving the carpets. There were some 230 knots to the inch! All of them had runny noses, horrible coughs, and little in the way of warm clothing. They looked miserable. I have not gotten over that experience to this day, and have no use for Persian carpets, their beauty notwithstanding.

C DEL C

There is a very special organization of aerospace and airline CEOs called the Conquistadores del Cielo (CdelC). It was formed in 1937 and meets twice a year. The Spring Meeting is held at a different place each year, either in the States or in Europe.

The Fall Meeting is always held at the A-BAR-A Ranch in Wyoming, just over the Colorado border. The ranch includes some 300,000 acres and is a full-blown dude ranch.

The membership is limited to approximately 100 members, usually about six to ten guests (potential members), and a few staff. Everyone who is anyone in aerospace, defense or airlines is a member, or wants to be.

George Roberts was a member, and invited me to attend the Spring Meeting at the Wigwam Resort in Arizona in 1984. The meeting kicked off with a big cocktail party, and I was very impressed with all the CEOs there. For example, Boeing, Lockheed, Northrup, Raytheon, American Airlines, United, Southwest, Lufthansa, etc. One of the unwritten rules is that no member ever lists CdelC in their resume'.

Meeting attendees could play tennis, golf, horseback ride, or shoot skeet or trap. Every day ended with a cocktail party and fun dinner/ BBQ. It lasted three days and I really enjoyed it. So I was pleased, several months later, when George invited me to attend the Fall Meeting in Wyoming, which met just after Labor Day for three and a half days.

**George Roberts and I at a CdelC
Ranch Meeting in Wyoming, late 1980's.**

The Ranch is beautiful, set in a wooded valley with the North Platt River coursing through the property. Made up of rustic cabins, dining room, pool, 9-hole golf course, and horses, it provides members an opportunity to socialize, talk privately, and not be worried about reporters. Activities ran from "fast draw pistol shooting" to fly fishing, golf, tennis, rifle shooting, horse shoes, tactical rifle shooting (1000 yards) and others. A veritable "big boys" camp. Guests can participate in as many or few of the activities as you may choose. Event winners get a nice trophy at the banquet on the last night, and you can bet there was plenty of competition with a bunch of

CEOs around! Several dinners are held on the banks of "Big Creek" and up at "Slim's Draw" for a BBQ at 9,000 feet.

George put me up for membership, and I was elected in 1987. An encouraging insight was that in order to qualify for membership in CdelC, "you had to be a CEO or, be in line to be CEO."

Until he died, George and I always bunked together.

FLY FISHING

For a number of years, the club had a special membership class called Fiesta Members, who did not have to be in the aerospace, defense, or airline industries. It was done away with, and the Fiesta members were absorbed into the regular membership. One year, George and I were in a cabin for four. We were bunked with the CEO of Security Pacific Bank in Los Angeles, Carl Hartnack. As I mentioned earlier, fly fishing was available at the Ranch, either on the North Platte or Big Creek.

One day I returned to our cabin. Carl had all this stuff lying on his bunk. I asked what he was doing, and he said, "I'm going fly fishing." I watched him put his gear together, and when he was ready he asked if I wanted to go along.

"Sure!" I said. I had never been fly fishing before.

We went to the river, where Carl waded out and made his cast. I watched from the bank. It was a lovely day, and as I stood there a flock of Canadian geese flew by and landed in a nearby meadow. Pintail ducks were in abundance as well, honking and having a great time! A Kingfisher scolded us from a tree. I was taken by the serenity of the whole scene; the river burbling by and the sun lighting up the pines and reflecting off the water.

Carl's casts were slow, measured and graceful. I found the whole experience rather spiritual. I decided then and there that I would take up fly fishing. And I did!

While it was very difficult to get a reservation at the ranch due to high demand, on several occasions I arranged times for Paul and Joan to come up for the weekend before the meeting and enjoy the "ranch life."

At home, Joan and I frequented our favorite watering holes on weekends in Rancho Bernardo. One such place was the Rancho Bernardo Inn, which was close to home. We often had dinner and then enjoyed the music in the bar. It was a lot of fun after a long day at the grove. I took her there for our 25th anniversary, and surprised her with a new, larger diamond for her engagement ring! We also enjoyed Bernardo's, a French restaurant that was also close and many of our friends were always there.

THE GREASY SPOON AWARD

Our Pacific Group Executive, Bill Rutherford, sponsored an annual competition among the group companies called the "Greasy Spoon Award." For Profit Plan meetings the Pacific Group Executives visited each company in the group for one to two days to listen to the company's plans in some detail. The second Profit Plan Meeting was usually when the competition was held, and it was an "in house" luncheon for the group executives.

I suspect that the group folks got tired of the usual fare offered by the companies, and reached for "bigger and better" for at least one meal from each company during the Profit Plan cycle. The winner received a "Golden Spoon," and the loser (worst company in the group), was given the "Greasy Spoon." We never wanted that, and always tried to put on a nice lunch for them. It was a matter of some pride that each group executive supported his companies for the best lunch/golden spoon, and to avoid, at all costs, the greasy spoon.

At some point, I decided that we would go for the Golden Spoon. We organized a magnificent lunch! We served the works: tamales, tacos, Spanish rice and beans, corn tortillas and ice cold Corona and Dos Equis beer in the conference room.

The pièce de résistance, however, was a pretty Mexican dancer that we brought in to provide live entertainment. We also provided the wooden floor for her stomping while she played her castanets. She was accompanied by three guitarists in full costume. OLE!

It was a fantastic lunch! We won the Golden Spoon. Interestingly, after our winning performance Bill cancelled further competitions. He probably figured it had "gone too far" …ya think?

Here is another comment about Bill Rutherford. The Continental Motor Companies were in his group. One such company, the General Products Company, was based in Muskegon, Michigan and manufactured diesel engines for the U.S. Army's M-60 Tank. The company owned a nice piece of property next to a lake. Bill had a conference center built, complete with electronics for presentations etc., the purpose of which was to hold group profit plan meetings there. Group companies had to trek to Muskegon for Profit Plan meetings when they were scheduled there.

In addition, he built a very nice lodge on the property. Four bedrooms with baths, and in the middle of the lodge was a large, well-furnished "family room" with TV, fireplace, and bar. This is where the group executives stayed for several weeks during profit plans. The visiting troops, us, stayed in more "rustic" cabins without such comforts. We could not help but notice as well, that there was a pier on the lake with boats tied up along with fishing gear. Anyone for Muskie and Northern Pike between profit plans meetings?

In the early 1980s, I brought Sharon Ramstad aboard as my assistant. She had experience at Ryan, a great personality and the skills to help me. We worked together for many years, and I am forever in her debt for looking after me through thick and thin!

A CHANGE OF PLANS

Around 1984 it became clear, given Joan's health, that the grove would not be an option for our later years. She had trouble with the heat there, and would really rather stay at our existing home. Given the company's growth and associated travel demands, the grove was becoming a lot more difficult for me as well. I considered keeping the grove and hiring a grove manager, but after talking to several of them, I wasn't comfortable. So, we decided to sell.

I called Gene Gillette, our land broker, and asked him about listing the grove. He told me that he thought it was worth $16,000/acre based on neighboring groves and the market. I told him that was nuts! I understood land owners thinking theirs is "the best," but I could actually back it up. We put money into infrastructure such as a three-inch water meter, a drainage system, and a fence around the property. Our fertilizer injection and drip irrigation systems were first rate and well-placed in the grove, as were "improved" grove roads. But most important, the grove was producing early and with significant quality and quantity of fruit from several popular varieties. Unfortunately, today I don't have the production numbers or price per pound records, but they were impressive!

Gene was stuck on his opinion, so I decided to market the property myself. I thought it was worth at least $20,000/acre. I put together a brochure on the property complete with detailed information and pictures and ran ads. An oil and gas lawyer from Montana called me about it, and asked if his representative could come by and look. He did, and liked what he saw! We sold it for $460,000... $20,000/ acre!

After the sale closed, the buyer's agent told me that the grove was "underpriced at $20,000 an acre!" I miss the grove to this day. It was really hard work, but I found it an excellent relief valve from the stresses of work, and I loved watching it grow and flourish. It was always a thrill to grow avocados commercially. I found it comforting to know you could make money working with Mother Nature... and having nothing to do with the stock market!

WHAT'S NEXT?

Once the APN-218 was in production and being installed in the B-52 and KC-135 fleets, we started looking for more applications. Both the B-52s and KC-135s belonged to SAC. A possible opportunity was getting the radar aboard C-130 Aircraft. The Air Force had over 800 of the aircraft in active and reserve fleets. The C-130's belonged to the USAF Military Airlift Command (MAC), located at Scott Air Force Base in Illinois.

When we met to discuss installing the APN-218 in the C-130 with the various USAF organizations involved, we ran into a problem. MAC did not have any development funds for installing new navigation equipment, even though the existing Doppler radar currently in the aircraft was a poor performer and seldom used by the air crews. The APN-218 was managed by Warner Robbins Air Logistics Central (WRALC). This turned out to be very convenient for us. While the C-130 Avionic Managers at WRALC were interested in replacing the existing Doppler with ours, they also lacked the funds to pay for a new installation design.

Installing APN-218 was not a simple matter. It was a much different design than the existing Doppler. While the mechanical and electrical interfaces with the aircraft were different, the most difficult challenge was the mechanical installation. The C-130 aircraft has a pressurized interior cabin. The aircraft actually had two skins. The outer skin and the inner skin formed the pressure vessel that created the pressurized interior/cabin.

The mechanical design of the APN-218 had to provide exposure of the radar's antenna to the outside world, and still be airtight in its connection to the aircraft.

BUT...NO FUNDS

Both MAC and WRALC were interested, but could not fund the necessary development and design work for the APN-218's installation. We were willing and able to do the design on our own. But when we approached Lockheed Aircraft Company in Marietta, Georgia, about giving us access to the aircraft drawings required for the design, Lockheed demurred, telling us they would not guarantee the aircraft structure's air worthiness unless they did the design!

That was a show stopper. Frankly, if I were them I would have done exactly the same thing. The old saw "necessity is the mother of invention" certainly worked for us. We came up with a great idea. What if we could convince Big Safari to install the APN-218 in its Spook C-130's, therefore paying for the installation drawings?

Big Safari was a USAF Aircraft System Development (ASD) Program, located at Wright-Patterson AFB. It was responsible for the design and development of USAF Reconnaissance Aircraft, most of which is classified, including the budget! This included both C-135 and C-130 type aircraft. By this time the Air Force was already operating modified RC, WC and EC-135 aircraft with our APN-218, and they were happy with its performance!

I had met and become friends with the Big Safari Commanding Officer during the B-1 Bomber Program. We decided to offer them a "free" APN-218 for their C-130's if they would have it installed by Lockheed Air Service (LAS). LAS did all the unique modifications to the C-130's for the USAF and foreign governments. The Big Safari leadership agreed to the arrangement. We were in the C-130. Wow!

LIFE IS *REALLY* GOOD!

Once all the non-recurring costs for the APN-218 C-130 installation was covered by Big Safari, both MAC and Warner Robbins decided to procure and install the system on all the USAF active and reserve aircraft. We sold another 700 radars! This brought the total of APN-218 Radars sold to over 2,000. TRE eventually manufactured and sold over 2,500 units, making it by far the company's largest and most profitable product.

I can't say enough about our engineers on this program. I would especially like to point out the terrific effort by Sparky who kept the program straight and level for a number of years! Well done! He was my second hire when I came aboard. A damn good pick!

THE WINDS OF CHANGE

In late April, 1984, Roy came to see me. He was never one for small talk and opened up the conversation by saying that I was to be the new president of Teledyne Ryan Aeronautical! What?!

I was totally taken aback. I had never even thought about it, and never saw it coming. Roy went on to say that the current president had not solved the APACHE Helicopter production problems, among other things, and that he had been removed.

I don't recall Roy asking me if I would accept the new job or not. He just went on like I had accepted it. He also said that I would continue to have responsibility for TRE, at least for the time being!

NOT AN EASY CALL

I was confused, to put it mildly. On the one hand, it was difficult to even think about leaving TRE. I had spent 12 years building it up to a $70M company with $10M net income, superior cash flow, a growing backlog. I had also worked hard to hire a first class management and technical staff, and assemble a cooperative and productive work force. Why would I want to take over a company that had lost $11M in net income on sales of $98M? I also knew the company was struggling mightily to get the APACHE Helicopter line going before its customer cancelled it for breach of contract.

Furthermore, you could write what I knew about helicopters on one fingernail. But you could also have said that about my knowledge of microwave and Doppler Radars at TRE! The whole idea was crazy… so I took the job!

I went home, poured two stiff drinks for Joan and me, sat down, and told her about "our" new job.

When the announcement came out (dated April 19, 1984), it was different than I remembered Roy telling me. No surprise there. The release said, "Hudson B. Drake, President of Teledyne Ryan Electronics, has been named President of Teledyne Ryan, comprised of Teledyne Ryan Aeronautical and Teledyne Ryan Electronics, which will continue as separate units."

No doubt, this was going to be really interesting!

CHAPTER EIGHT

Teledyne Ryan Aeronautical: 1984-1988

I drove down to Teledyne Ryan Aeronautical (TRA) the following day to see Bill Rutherford. He and the other group executives were housed on the second floor, immediately adjacent to the main gate and lobby. Claude Ryan's old office was on the first floor, and all TRA presidents since had "ruled" from there.

Bill had set up a temporary office for me just outside the group offices. I didn't want to office there for several reasons. First, while it was quiet, it was isolated from the factory. Second, I didn't want to be near the group executives, and finally, I wanted to be with "my troops." I established my new office on the second floor, way north of the main gate, between the legal department and the project manager's offices. My new digs had a fine view of San Diego bay and were close to the APACHE manufacturing building, machine shop and the FIREBEE Target manufacturing area, which was closed at the time for lack of business.

There was a "new sheriff in town" and I wanted to look out my office window and see APACHE's coming off the production line. I wanted to enjoy the hustle and bustle of a high-end manufacturing plant with all its associated activity and excitement!

You may recall from earlier chapters, criticism of both Vice Presidents Humphrey and Agnew for bringing their staffs to their new job in the Executive Branch of government. In my move from TRE, I brought only my assistant. I was determined to work with the talent that was there, unless I found it lacking.

Sharon Ramstad (I called her "Sharona") worked with me as an assistant for years. She was widowed when we were at TRE, but she had three fine children who helped fill in the gap. She was always smiling and had something good to say about everyone. She was patient with me, and fortunately, shared most of my sense of humor. She always looked out for me.

I knew both Chuck McGill, the Vice President of Finance, and his Controller, Arden Honrud, and I liked them both. They became key members of my team. Our finance people dealt a great deal with the corporate office financial folks, and both of these men were highly respected there. Arden was TRA's version of the Sphinx. He rarely smiled or said much and was a real stoic. Arden always had a half smoked cigar clamped in his teeth. He was another long term employee. He was capable, efficient, and everyone liked him.

I brought in Glenn Rich to head Marketing in 1985. He was a nice enough fellow, and presented himself well with a good background. However, he was simply ineffective. I let him go shortly thereafter. Hiring a professional is an art form, and you can only do so much diligence sorting someone out. So you hire him or her and hope that it works. If it does, "good for you!" if it doesn't, don't just fret about it… "Act!" Another life lesson.

TRA was located next to San Diego's Lindbergh Field. It covered over 40 acres and had one million sq. ft. under roof. There was a paint shop at one end, and a hanger for our planes at the other. It definitely was not TRE! The Aeronautical side of the house dominated sales for the company, which were significantly larger than the Electronics Company. It was crystal clear to me that my mission, first and foremost, was to get the APACHE production line going and supporting the ever increasing delivery schedule. Period!

THE APACHE

As I am going to be talking a lot about it, what exactly is the Army's AH-64A Advanced Attack APACHE Helicopter?

This weapon system is generally agreed to be the most awesome anti-tank/anti-personnel fighting machine ever built! From the beginning of its development program, The APACHE was designed to live, operate, and be maintained under battlefield conditions with a minimum of field support equipment and technical personnel.

Its mission is to provide concentrated anti-tank and suppressive firepower on targets in day, night and adverse weather conditions. Its maximum forward speed is 196 MPH with a range of 800 miles. It has twin engines, and can fly in total darkness or poor weather and still strike targets. It carries 16 Hellfire missiles, a laser-guided weapon capable of destroying the heaviest tanks with a single hit. Alternately, it can carry 2.75" rocket pods for use against lighter targets. It also has a 30mm Chain Gun automatic cannon capable of firing up to 600 rounds per minute. This is mounted under the fuselage for ground target suppression.

The APACHE had gone through ten years of engineering design, development and testing by Army and industry teams. Teledyne Ryan Aeronautical was chosen by Hughes Helicopter, the prime contractor, in 1973 to provide engineering services and to build the airframes for two flight prototypes. These were to be evaluated by the Army in a competitive fly-off with a design produced by another industry team. The Hughes-TRA team won! Hughes was then acquired by the McDonnell Douglas Corporation. Nothing changed contractually for us, we just had a new Prime Contractor.

When you think about the APACHE and what we did at TRA, consider that everything you see except the rotor blades and rubber tires... we build!

On January 26, 1984, the U.S. Army accepted the first production APACHE model. I was brought aboard on April 19, 1984, three months later and just weeks after turning 49.

The APACHE, AH-64A ATTACK HELICOPTER

THE CHALLENGE

So, let me set the stage. The challenge we now faced was to move the company from building several "prototypes" to "production" helicopters at a designated rate per month. The delivery schedule moved quickly, from 1-2 per month, to 3 per month. TRA couldn't get past one, and that "one" was being hand built, which is to say it was not really a "product" of the assembly line in its current setup. So, there you have it.

I called Tony Richards, my Vice President of Manufacturing, into my office.

"What's the problem…why aren't we delivering?" I asked.

He listed a number of things that had been done. He was convinced that the "table was now set" and our rate would go up this month! I had known Tony for a long time. He was a good guy and had worked at TRA for many years. He was knowledgeable and had a positive personality. Tony was a Captain in the naval reserve, and held a degree in Industrial Engineering from Penn State. Every one respected him, and so did I.

I asked if he was sure that the problem wasn't in procurement or support. Were we short of purchased or in-house made parts? Were there enough people, and did the people we have possess the right skills? He said no to all that. The problem was in the assembly line, and he felt it was fixed.

"OK, let's hope you're right." I said.

I spent a lot of time wandering around the plant opening doors, talking to the work force, union (UAW) stewards, line supervisors and workers. We also had a number of Vietnam Veterans working on APACHE under a special government program. I worked my way through engineering, program management, quality, purchasing, manufacturing, human resources and yes, the safety and nurse's offices.

There was a lot of heavy machinery in use at the plant, and lost time accidents had always been a concern, especially here and now. The company had invested serious money in a CNC (computer-numerically controlled) 5-axis, 3-spindle, 90' bed profiler from Cincinnati Milacron. Most tolerances on APACHE machined parts were 5/1000 of an inch.

Such tolerances were necessary to produce the alignment tolerance for the total airframe required for the inter-relationship between the navigation equipment, Target Acquisition and Designation System, Pilot's Night Vision System, and the weapons attach points. For assembly purposes, the fuselage was divided into four sub-assemblies: forward, center, aft, and tail boom. Each sub-assembly had a structure fixture for framing, longerons, skinning etc. The sub-assemblies were mated together in a mating fixture and then moved to a final alignment fixture. Based on the original planning material, at a high rate of production, and a multi-shift operation, flow time per air frame would be from six to eight weeks. The fuselage had ten stations, and there were ten more stations for the wings, nacelles, vertical and horizontal stabilator, and so on.

Assembly of the fuselage was a real challenge. It was made up of 7,200 parts, held together by 85,000 specialty fasteners and rivets.

SUMMONED TO CORPORATE

I had been on the job no more than five or six weeks when Roy called and told me Henry wanted to see me. I knew that Henry had to be unhappy, but I wasn't sure about what. There was plenty to bitch about. Roy, myself, and Chuck flew up to corporate and walked into Henry's corner office, overlooking the Los Angeles

Country Club. He stood up and came around his desk to stand in front of me. He was a good four inches taller than I was, and he seemed to tower over me.

His face was crimson.

"Where's my cash? You're destroying Teledyne's Quarterly results all by yourself!" When he spoke, no, shouted this, saliva sprayed from his mouth…

I thought to myself *Surely he knows I'm brand new in the job, and had little to do with the cash flow problem.* Except, he knew I was aware that the cash crunch was because of our dismally-behind delivery schedule, and that the $2M a copy for the APACHEs wasn't going into Teledyne's till per our profit plan, because we weren't delivering! All I could say was that we were committed to solving the delivery problems and were doing everything we could to bring it about at the earliest possible time. No one else said a word.

Henry turned away and returned to his desk. The meeting was over. Although there was no visible blood, my ears rang with his message.

ELUSIVE ANSWERS

My main focus, as you might imagine, stayed on the APACHE production line. I spent hours during all three shifts walking the line, looking for possible reasons for our slow delivery rate. What was it that was holding us up?

I concentrated on the four major fuselage stations as the probable source of our production delays. I looked at man hours per station, material, flow times, overtime, skill levels, quality (squawks), training, etc. Nothing stood out. Our production problem was insidious! As the days turned into weeks without answers, I became more and more concerned. Despite Tony's continued assurances, nothing had really changed. We were still only producing one airframe per month versus a schedule requirement of three…and we were falling further and further behind.

I had two major concerns.

First and foremost was the fear of being declared "in default" and having our contract cancelled. The second, was wondering how much time I had left to find a solution?

When I arrived at TRA, there was a "two tier" wage program in effect on the APACHE production line. This situation was brought about by the fact that we had very few assemblers, and the ones we had were at the top of the wage structure due to their seniority.

We were forced to hire and train new assemblers, and the union agreed that we could hire at the lower end of the entry level wage in order to staff the program. The entry rate was about $5.00 an hour lower than scale. Such a situation had consequences, as you might expect. After a relatively short time, the new hires would leave the company for higher wages elsewhere, creating a turnover problem for us.

Further, after a few months, workers would demand wage increases. This was another de-stabilizing issue on the line. It certainly wasn't helping our efforts to increase deliveries. To resolve this issue, we established an "evaluation program" wherein if the employee could pass a test, they could qualify for a wage increase. I called an all hands meeting in the Plaza area, between the main office building and the APACHE assembly building, and made the announcement. It was well received, and solved our wage problem.

A number of the new hires were Vietnam veterans, many whom could not find work upon returning to civilian life. The government asked industry to reach out to these men and women and give them employment. TRA answered the call, and we put over 200 veterans to work on the APACHE line.

I felt we were making some progress here and there, but fundamentally, the APACHE line hadn't changed since I arrived.

I still swam laps at home, but felt the pressure from work, and missed the more physical work at the avocado grove. I began jogging during the week. At lunch time, I drove from the office to either Harbor or Shelter Island where there were many good places to jog and enjoy the bay, sail boats and salt air. When I returned to my office, I would shower and be ready for the afternoon.

Another "perk" was the proximity of the Point Loma Seafood Market. It specialized In crab sandwiches and an outstanding fish plate. We used it a lot, not only for our own benefit, but for customer entertaining as well. We also used Lubach's Restaurant, the Westgate Hotel and Mr. A's, for a really spectacular view of San Diego Bay and North Island when we did more serious entertaining.

One fun thing I often did, was to take a customer in the King Air, and fly to Catalina Island for a "Buffalo" burger lunch. Buffalo were raised there commercially and the burger was pretty good. The beauty of the trip was that I had the customers undivided attention. It was very effective. Another life lesson.

THE FIREBEE

One of Teledyne Ryan Aeronautical's core products has been the design and manufacture of the FIREBEE BGM-34S Target Drone, which we manufacture for all three services, and have for years. The Navy was, and is, our biggest customer. It is a radio controlled (line of sight) jet-powered target that is used for "real life" simulation of an enemy fighter aircraft. The drone flies effectively against both aircraft and ships. FIREBEE is capable of flying at altitudes up to 40,000 feet at a speed of 520 knots. Fighter pilots like to fly against it because it can hold altitude in a 5g turn, which replicates an enemy fighter. Unfortunately, however, it was long out of production.

The BGM-34S FIREBEE Target Drone

After my promotion to TRA, our Washington, D.C. office held a "Meet the New President" reception for our customers and supporters at a local hotel. It was well attended and it gave me a chance to meet a number of important people and customers.

While I was in Washington, I made an appointment with the Navy's program manager for targets. That man was Captain John Shulick, Director for Target Systems, Naval Air Systems Command. I asked him why the Navy wasn't buying more FIREBEE Targets? It had been three years since we had an order, and we delivered for a number of years at 60 to 70 per year. Was there an operational problem?

"No, not at all." He said, "In fact, I would like to order more because we really need them. We just don't have the budget."

Well, I thought, *that was good news.* But why didn't we know about his budget problem sooner?

I suggested that TRA prepare an unsolicited proposal for a multi-year buy of BGM-34S Targets, and in the interim, we would work the "Hill" to gather support for the buy from the appropriate committees of Congress, specifically those related to defense and appropriations. Captain Shulick was supportive. Taking the initiative, another life lesson.

Truthfully, we had excellent arguments. The fleet inventory was way down and a shortage of targets would seriously affect fleet readiness. It would limit the Navy's capability to adequately test emerging weapons and defense systems, especially with the needs of the new Aegis Cruiser, which was just joining the fleet.

We prepared and submitted our proposal in June 1984, just two months after my arrival at TRA. In due time we were awarded an $18.5M multi-year contract: 87 FIREBEES a year for three years! This is an extraordinary example of something that met both the

Navy's needs...and ours. And in a timely fashion! It also proves again that you need to get off your butt and call on your customer... regularly! Someone in marketing at Ryan had clearly been asleep at the switch! Another life lesson.

The FIREBEE 34-S used a Teledyne CAE J-69 engine and included wiring and assemblies from TRE as well. Value added! When we re-opened the FIREBEE Line, I was all over it. Our employees were thrilled with the start of the new line after a three-year hiatus. It was a big morale booster plant-wide!

I decided that it was time to bring something down to TRA that I did at TRE...an open house. As I said earlier, nothing gets a manufacturing plant floor cleaner than when you declare an "open house" and wives and kids are invited to "see where dad works"! The shop floor never looked better, not a chip in sight, all the safety lines around the various machine tools were freshly painted and everything was in its place. The real reason, of course, was giving families a chance to see what we produce at TRA, including sub-contract work. Besides hot dogs, hamburgers, ice cream, drinks and all the trimmings, on exhibit was a "full-up" APACHE Attack Helicopter, a FIREBEE Target, F-18 Fighter, plus some RPV's and special exhibits. A huge hit with everyone!

SAN SALVADOR

Something else was going on in 1985, in the small country of San Salvador (SS) in Central America. The country was plagued by violence and poverty due to overpopulation, class struggles, and politics. Civil war broke out in 1980. It was the U.S.-backed government versus the Farabundo Marti National Liberation Front (FMNLF). Death and destruction were the daily fare. Bridges were blown up, churches sacked, people raped and murdered, and fields burned. A U.S. Army General and friend from my Washington days was there. He heard I was now at Ryan Aeronautical, which was famous for reconnaissance drones in Vietnam, and invited me to come down and see him.

He wanted to talk.

I went, and he told me that the U.S. Army was flying a "toy" recon-naissance RPV[3] trying to find enemies in the jungle. He was having to send his troops into the jungle looking for the RPV's because they frequently crashed and he needed to recover the payload of cameras and film. He was very frustrated. He asked if I could do anything about his situation.

"Let me talk to my people." I said.

THE MODEL 410

I brought my technical people together, and we brainstormed the San Salvador problem. We had already been thinking about what might make sense for a small capable RPV in both military and com-mercial markets. There were some distinct possibilities. There were applications for a low cost drone in plenty of fields, such as border patrol, anti-smuggling, search and rescue, and so on. We felt the best answer for SS was a new RPV: the 410. It had to be simple to maintain, capable of operations during all-weather and day/night conditions. It also needed to have endurance, a low operational cost, a long range, and the ability to carry a variety of payloads.

The 410 would be powered by a pusher propeller, meaning the engine sits at the rear of the aircraft. It would reach a top speed of

---

3   RPV stands for Remote Piloted Vehicle

190 knots, and have a payload compartment that could handle 24 cubic feet.

The prototype was rolled out in August 1987. The bad news was that my friend had been transferred, but more to the point, the U.S. was losing interest in its support of SS. They had no desire to upgrade our drawings to military-specification so that they could purchase the aircraft. There was also a raft of other requirements which would have to be met in order to sell to our military.

However, if you had what the military needed, when they needed it, they always found a way to get it done! Commercial opportunities were plentiful, and our team pressed on with flight tests. We used a pilot until everything was checked out, then we would go unmanned.

Flight testing before droning the 410

DO SOMETHING!

Meanwhile, back at the APACHE assembly line there was no improvement. At this point, I felt that I had two choices. One, of course, was to continue trying (without much promise) and wait for the axe to fall. Two, do something! As you can probably guess, I decided on number two.

I phoned our customer, the president of the McDonnell Douglas Corporation in St. Louis, Missouri. When I was put through I explained who I was, and asked to come and see him.

"Of course," He said. "When would you like to come?"

"Tomorrow." Why waste time, right?

I scheduled the company Lear Jet and was airborne early the next morning for Lambert Field in St. Louis. I can't remember the president's entire name, but his first name was Bob.

He welcomed me and after chatting a few minutes I plunged into what was going on at TRA's APACHE assembly line. Or not going on, as the case was. I told him everything we had done, that nothing had helped, and that we were stumped. I asked for his help. Bob was quiet for a minute or so.

"Our senior vice president for manufacturing, Herb Perlmutter, retired last year. I think he could help you, would you be interested in him?" He finally said.

I felt like jumping up and down, but kept my professional demeanor.

"Herb's help would be an incredible asset!" I responded.

I thanked him profusely and prepared to leave. Before I could go, Bob asked if I would like to have a quick tour of his factory.

I said, "Absolutely."

A gentleman took me out on the factory mezzanine where you could look out at the floor. There was an ocean of milling machines, five-axis, four-axis and three-axis etc. It was an amazing sight.

I flew home, very satisfied with my decision to reach out and, "do something." Another life lesson.

Herb arrived from St. Louis, settled in, and joined me in analyzing the various assembly line stations. We checked on all three shifts. He was a real manufacturing classic, having spent years in charge of large fighter aircraft production lines. He was delightful to work with; easy going and personable, but didn't miss a thing. Unfortunately, he didn't see any obvious problems in our line either!

Finally, after extensive analysis and discussion we settled on what we "thought" was the key to our production line's problem: the Center Mate Station. It was just behind the Forward Assembly, and just in front of the Aft Tail Boom Assembly.

It is a complex station and we concluded that the problem wasn't something wrong with our existing line per se, it was that we needed to build a second Center Mate Station for the line to perform efficiently and to-schedule. We worked the numbers and thought it would cost about $5M. Above and beyond the $5M, there was another, much larger and more significant number that I had to deal with. I was negative in cash flow to the tune of $60M! Now you can appreciate why Henry was so upset at our earlier meeting!

A CRITICAL TRIP TO CORPORATE

Imagine my concern of having to go to see George or, especially, Henry with a request for even more money. The request would require Henry's approval regardless. I remembered my first APACHE related trip earlier in my tenure, which I certainly had not forgotten.

By this time, I had also learned that Pacific Group Executives were always "busy" with other "important" matters when there was "heavy news" to deliver to corporate. Both Bill and Roy opted out of this trip, and I went alone, which was fine with me.

As I recall, only George and Henry were in Henry's office when I arrived, though Charlie Rinsch, the corporate finance czar, might have been there too. At least this trip I got to sit down. Better than standing like last time!

I told them the story of my trip to St. Louis, and the McDonnell's president making Herb Perlmutter available to me. I expressed as best I could what the two of us had studied, the result of our analysis, and our conclusion. We needed a second Center Mate Station, and it would cost $5M. There were some questions from Henry which I answered, and then without too much drama Henry said, "OK."

I thanked him and said we would do everything possible to get the new station up and going quickly. Whew, what a relief!

There was no need for Herb to wait until the new station was on line, so he left for Missouri with my admiration and thanks.

SUCCESS

We got the new station up and going in record time it. It became clear very quickly that it was going to solve our problem. All the assemblers settled into the new flow and things just came together smoothly.

We quickly moved to two airframes per month and then three… and over the next several years met our contract maximum of 12 per month! We ultimately produced over 1000 APACHE Airframes! At peak tooling and production, we had 600 direct people, plus 100 or so indirect support on the APACHE line. I was a relieved and happy man. I had two active and successful production lines: the FIREBEE Line and (finally) APACHE! Damn, life is good!

Celebrating the delivery of APACHE Airframe No. 100 to the U.S. Army, in the Plaza in front of Don Lebow's wall artwork, 1986

There is an important lesson to be learned from our APACHE problem, and how it was solved. To wit, as a leader, don't be afraid to admit you don't know all the answers. It is not a weakness. When the situation warrants, ask for help. Your people will respect you and you might be surprised at how much helpful advice you get! Another life lesson.

I wrote letters of appreciation to both Bob and Herb. No one could ask for better support than they provided.

APACHE Final Assembly

As you might expect, I am very proud of the APACHE helicopter program, both the military men and women who fly them and the folks that built them here in San Diego. There are many technical advances in the helicopter, but none more important, to me, than what I will call the bow beam.

One of the major design objectives the army wanted in the APACHE was a solution to the biggest killer of attack helicopter crews: roll-overs, which crushed them. In the APACHE, we designed a roll cage around the cockpit that protected the crew from the deadly rollover. The cockpit was tiered so that the pilot could see over the gunner in front of him. A 30-degree aluminum casting called a "bow beam", or frame, was installed in front of the gunner, and another one was installed behind the pilot. Both beams were integral to the roll cage. The bow beams were exceedingly difficult to build, given the very tight tolerances involved in fitting and securing the cockpit canopy windows with the beams and the fuselage. It took time and effort to solve, but we did. The really good news is that to the best of my knowledge and belief, there has never been a crew fatality associated roll over!

If you build'em, you gotta fly 'em!

TAKING CARE OF BUSINESS

Before I leave the APACHE Program, I must relate a story. Under our form of government, doing business with the Department of Defense (and other departments of course) can be challenging, especially when Congress gets involved.

The APACHE Helicopter Program, like all DoD programs is typically funded annually. This means every fiscal year you have to keep a sharp eye out to insure that your program(s) will be supported not only by the DoD, but by those with the money: Congress. In the Congress, you have to know key committee members and their staffs as they relate to your business.

I was fortunate that California's Senator, Alan Cranston (D), was on the Armed Service Committee, a very important committee for our business. We contacted him and his staff on at least an annual basis, and usually more often regarding programs of interest to us and California. My main man in Washington was Carl Bayer, who ran our office there. I phoned him and asked him to set up a meeting for me with Senator Cranston to talk about the APACHE Helicopter program funding. Carl called back and told me that his office declined to meet with me! I was shocked. We employed about 1,000 people on the APACHE Program! We're in California…what was up with our Senator?

I pulled out my Congressional Record Book and looked up Senator Cranston and what committees he sat on. Bingo! He was also on the Veterans Affairs Committee.

I asked Carl to set up a meeting for me with him for Veterans Affairs, as TRA was the largest employer of veterans in the country, with over 220 on the APACHE line! Carl set it up and I met with the Senator. Of course, I mentioned what a fine job the vets were doing for the country on the APACHE assembly line, and that they would appreciate his support for the funding of the APACHE Helicopter Program in the coming year. The senator was delighted to provide his support! An important life lesson is to remember the old adage "there is more than one way to skin a cat."…especially in Washington, D.C.!

I made another management change during the push to solve the APACHE problem, Tony Richards. As I said earlier, Tony was a solid citizen and tried his very best in a very difficult situation. He was right, the problem was in the assembly line. Unfortunately, he couldn't get his finger on it. While I brought in Bill Cassidy to run manufacturing, I asked Tony to help us in marketing. He has an engaging personality, technical smarts, and unsurpassed experience in all our products. We needed senior help there. Tony was not happy about it, but over time, he came to enjoy it and did a fine job. He especially seemed to shine at major shows, like the Paris Air Show.

I also brought Don LeBow, the artist who did the work for me at TRE, down to TRA. We had a really big exterior wall that faced a large plaza in the middle of the factory area. I wanted him to paint a TRA history of Lindbergh's Spirit of St. Louis (which Ryan designed and built), RPV's from the Vietnam era, and, of course, APACHE and FIREBEE. Again, Don excelled. See picture on p. 176 if you missed it.

It wasn't long before another issue appeared. It seemed we had a drug problem in manufacturing, and especially in and around the APACHE line.

When I heard about it, I went for one of my walks around the factory, stopping and talking to union members, supervision, maintenance personnel, and others. No one was saying "yes," but they were saying enough… we definitely had something going on. Another indicator was something I always kept an eye on: lost time accidents. They were going up. I called the San Diego Police Department and told them what I thought was going on. They sent over a young man and woman, whom we hired and badged, and put them on the line. Just ten days later we had the pushers.

One of their favorite hangouts was a FIREBEE shipping container (probably 15' by 8'). They had cut holes in the ceiling to let the smoke out, and spent their afternoons kicked back. I'm sure it beats riveting helicopter parts!

In 1986, Captain Shulick came for the roll-out of the first FIREBEE production unit. There was a big crowd, and everyone was very proud. The view from my office window was getting a lot better too!

Capt. John Shulick and I by the first re-ordered FIREBEE Target drone delivery - 1986

A NEW PRESIDENT AT TRE

Bill Rutherford had installed Bob Steenberge as my replacement at TRE. Bob had run another Pacific Group Company, and Bill brought him to San Diego. I found it interesting that Bill had named Bob president of a company for which I was responsible… and I had never met the man! I had lots to do at TRA, so I didn't get by TRE very often to check up on things at my old stomping grounds. It's possible I didn't want to go back there because there were times I wished I'd never left…! No, that's not true. I relished the job at TRA.

Bob was a nice guy, but very technical. He avoided eye contact and had a disconcerting habit of always stroking his beard.

I figured that Bill felt TRE had a strong enough business base to last two or three years, affording Bob time to develop new products. Instead, and most unfortunately, Bob developed a bleeding ulcer which laid him low. He returned to TRE briefly before he transferred to another company, but not in line management.

LAND OF THE PHARAOHS

Beyond the FIREBEE and APACHE Helicopter legs to my story at TRA, there is a "third leg," the SCARAB Program. Shortly after my arrival at TRA, I learned about another possible program in the works. This possibility would come from Egypt.

In early 1983, Bill Rutherford and family took a vacation trip to London and then on to Cairo, Egypt, as they had never been there before. They were met by the local agent/consultants to several of our Teledyne Companies, including Teledyne Ryan.

Retired Egyptian Air Force (EAF) Generals El Sayed Ali Nadim and Sayed Maged Aly, were the principals of Sahara Overseas Services (SOS). Over the course of their stay, General Nadim asked Bill about possible new business for SOS in Egypt, and specifically, about drones/RPVs. Bill, of course, was knowledgeable from his Ryan days, and gave them a tutorial.

Some weeks after Bill's return, he got a call from General Nadim in Cairo. The General told Bill that he had spoken with Field Marshall Abu Ghazala, and he was interested in the idea of RPVs! TRA sent some engineers to Cairo to work with the EAF on developing a new intelligence, surveillance and reconnaissance (ISR) RPV program.

At the June 1983 Paris Air Show, the Field Marshall was briefed at the Teledyne Chalet on "possibilities." One of the big problems addressed was that the EAF had no C-130 type aircraft to use as launch vehicles for RPVs, as the U.S. Air Force had. An Egyptian system would have to be an integrated ground Launch Recovery Vehicle (LRV). The RPV would launch from a trailer with a booster rocket that could be jettisoned. It would then be recovered by parachute equipped with deployable air bags on the bottom of the aircraft to absorb landing impact.

The design reflected a Dupont Kevlar reinforced epoxy fuselage, 12' wings, 20' length, a range of 1400 nautical miles, a payload of 250 pounds, a speed of 0.8 Mach and a ceiling of 43,000 feet. It would be powered by a Teledyne CAE 373-8 jet engine with a 970 pound thrust, similar to the Harpoon Missile engine which CAE manufactured. The gross weight was 2,400 pounds.

The Egyptians named the RPV "SCARAB," a religious symbol of resurrection. We came to a preliminary agreement in June of 1984. SOS played a significant role, making sure our team understood the local business practices, language, and customs of Egyptians and the EAF, which smoothed the whole process.

I signed the definitive contract on October 29, 1984. It called for 29 RPVs, three LRV's and three sets of Ground Support Equipment. A significant accomplishment of our engineers was that they managed to pack all the key electronics (GPS, Flight Control System, communications etc.) into an area smaller than a 50-gallon drum. The EAF sent seven representatives to TRA to form a resident team. It was headed by Colonel Hafez Zaki (PhD). The representatives enjoyed San Diego. In time, several of them left their apartments near the plant and moved to Coronado Island…pretty nice indeed. Hafez was one of them.

I don't believe anybody thought that our partnership with the EAF was going to be a "walk in the park." Trust me, it wasn't.

The first major argument I had with Hafez was over the Inertial Navigation System (INS). He and the EAF wanted INS in SCARAB. However, it was not part of the contract. At least once in your life, you should navigate a negotiation with an Egyptian. The Egyptians have been "skinning" people for centuries. Their arguments are very emotional and endless, the facts notwithstanding. I looked into what impact it would have on us cost-wise, as well as the effect on the avionics suite (weight, power etc.). Engineering said it would not be a problem, and the cost was manageable as well.

I met with Hafez and told him that we would include the INS in the deal in the interest of getting the program off to a timely and positive start.

"However, this is a major concession on our part." I added. "There can't be any more. In addition, I'll no doubt need something from you "down the camel path" and I expect you to honor this debt."

He agreed.

PROBLEMS WITH "NO SEEUMS"

Let me turn to another, much larger problem. The mission the EAF planned for SCARAB was reconnaissance. It wasn't talked about, but SCARAB was designed from the "get go" to be stealthy with a low Radar Cross Section (RCS). RCS is a measure of how detectable an object is with radar, and is a property of the target reflectivity. A stealth aircraft is covert and will have design features that give it a low RCS, such as absorbent paint, flat surfaces, or surfaces specifically angled to reflect somewhere other than towards the source.

The Egyptian Government was extremely concerned with their neighbor to the West, Libya, and its leader, Muammar Ghaddafi. Libya, among other things, was always pushing border conflicts with both Egypt and Chad. It also was well armed, supplied, capable and boisterous. The EAF wanted to know (or "see" if you will), what was going on along the border with Libya, and further into Libya as well. With a low RCS, Libyan military radars would not be able to see SCARAB coming. Therefore, they would not be able to stop its mission... its payload would take precise pictures, and coupled with GPS could accurately depict situations and locate potential targets.

Several books could be written about the U.S. Government's requirements to allow the export of military type equipment and designs. For one, the Munitions Control Desk in the State Department is a formidable barrier. Without going into detail, we had a problem obtaining an export license, without which, there would be no SCARAB.

To drive home how stringent Munitions Control, the State Department, and export licenses could be, here's a story. When I was at TRE, I went to South Africa with Ted Trimmer from my marketing department. We called on the South African Air Force and briefed them on the capabilities of our Doppler Navigation System, the APN-220. The South African Air Force was also rolled into their police function when it related to airborne missions.

They were intrigued with the APN-220 because they had a serious problem with parts of the population growing marijuana up on the escarpments. The Great Escarpment in South Africa varies in altitude between 6,000 feet and 9,600 feet and runs close to the West and South coasts. It is a very challenging environment.

Our navigation system would allow them to safely fly helicopters in and around the peaks of the escarpment, and accurately locate illegal marijuana growing areas. South Africa wanted to buy 18 systems. We were delighted! When we got home, we prepared the appropriate paperwork for export and filed it with the State Department. It was returned approved. So far, so good.

We were ready to release manufacture of the radars to the factory floor when we received a letter from Munitions Control revoking State's approval. Apparently, Munitions Control felt that the South Africans would "harass the natives" with the Doppler equipped helicopters! What?! I couldn't believe it... but it was over!

WELCOME HELP

Frank Wisner was our ambassador to Egypt and a real professional. We enlisted his support to help us with our SCARAB export issue. I also contacted my very good friend, David Miller, who was a White House Fellow classmate, and later served as our ambassador to Tanzania and Zimbabwe. David was working in Washington, D.C. with a group involved in foreign affairs. Everybody pitched in to resolve the problem.

We soon learned that the "problem" was the SCARAB's RCS. It was so low that our own (U.S.) military radars could not pick it up or see it. They were understandably not happy. Our solution was to install a "corner reflector" in the leading edge of the wing.

This device is shaped like an L, and is carefully placed to ensure a degree of reflection with sufficient return to be "seen" by our radar. The American radar was much better than either Egypt's or Libya's. With our military now satisfied, the license was issued, and we were free to proceed with the program. Yes!

Of course I also wondered about the funding for the program. Who was paying for all this? I never found out, but I think it was AID money. Certainly, there were agencies in the U.S., not just Egypt, which would be quite interested in what Ghaddafi was up to.

THANK YOU VERY MUCH!

I was awarded the National Management Association's Gold Knight of Management in 1985-86 on the recommendation of both the Ryan Electronics and Aeronautical Management Associations. I was delighted. My brother flew in for the festivities from Dallas. It was wonderful to have him there. He passed away from undiagnosed prostate cancer shortly thereafter.

Celebrating the Gold Knight of Management Award with my family (left to right: brother, Lad, Son, Paul, my wife, Joan, son, Howard, niece, Barbie and her husband, Tom)

CAIRO

As mentioned earlier, Chuck McGill was my Vice President of Finance at TRA. He often traveled with me on trips to Egypt. He was short in stature, but an astute business man and good friend. We travelled well together, and he gave me good, seasoned advice. Chuck had a good sense of humor, and enjoyed a stiff drink. He and his wife, Pat, lived near us at home and we socialized often.

Travel to Egypt was relatively easy. Typically, I would fly to Paris, usually with Chuck. If I flew alone, I would fly to Geneva and connect with Chuck in Cairo. I liked the Geneva stop because it gave me a chance to catch up with Leo on Teledyne goings-on in Europe and the Mid- East... and, OK, maybe get a round of golf in at the Geneva Country Club!

Upon arrival in Cairo, we would be met by Nadim or one of his people at the airport and driven to our hotel, usually the Sheraton Heliopolis. Renting a car and driving in Cairo for us or any non-natives is a suicide mission. I can't begin to describe the traffic scene! Narrow stinky streets and alleys, sheep, camels, oxen, pedestrians, fumes, waste, junk…awful! The only rule was whether or not you could force the other guy to stop or turn before you collided. Pedestrians had no rights at all, and were legitimate targets.

The Sheraton was a nice place and, once out of the traffic, I was comfortable there. The rooms were decent and reasonably clean. The hotel was convenient to the SOS offices and visits to the EAF. The traditional breakfast was Foul (pronounced "fool"), which consists of fava beans with onions and tomatoes, and usually, pita bread. Also popular was Kashari, a mix of rice, lentils, and macaroni. Egyptian cuisine was conducive to a vegetarian diet, driven by the ready availability of various foods from local farms along the Nile River. Meat such as lamb was available and popular, but too expensive for the vast majority of Cairo's seven million inhabitants.

In Egypt, as time allowed, Nadim arranged travel for Chuck and I to visit most of the popular tourist sites.

AN OASIS

The Great Bitter Lake is a saltwater lake which is part of the Suez Canal. As the canal has no locks, seawater flows freely into the lake from the Mediterranean in the North and the Red Sea to the South. Egyptians of means bought property along the lake because it was a welcome respite from all the heat, pollution, and crowds of Cairo. It was about an hour and a half from Cairo by car. Perhaps the Egyptian's version of Camp David?

General Nadim owned a large lot there and built a four-story resort home for his family. He and his wife had the first floor, and each of the children had a floor of their own above. Chuck and I were there a number of times, and I think Norm visited there as well. It was very informal and we had lots of fun. Nadim also had a speedboat. We would take it out around some small islands and get a close look at the ships transiting the canal. He had enough property to have a decent sized garden as well.

At his request I brought him some avocado cuttings from my grove, and also some small grape vine cuttings. They did very well there.

As the "cradle of civilization," there were millennia-old monuments that sat along the Nile River valley, including the Colossal Pyramids and Sphinx at Giza, not to mention the hieroglyph-lined Karnac Temple and the Valley of the Kings in Luxor. All of it was extremely impressive.

With all due respect to the Egyptians, it's hard to correlate these ancient wonders with the destitution, broken infrastructure and smog of its capital, Cairo, the largest city in the country. One can't help but ask *What happened to these people?*

Many people are aware of the incredible engineering feats of the Ancients, and perhaps the pyramids in particular. At the largest pyramid, the Cheops, I had an inspiring experience. I climbed up the inside passage along with all the other tourists. It was hot in the passageway and the air was stale. As we ascended, it grew hotter. Upon arriving at the top, we were in the King's chamber with his sarcophagus. It was crowded and I ended up in a corner while our guide explained about the chamber. Suddenly, I became aware of a cool stream of fresh air which was blowing lightly on me. I looked around and up for the source. In the ceiling I spotted a small crevice, maybe eight or so inches long by two inches wide. The Ancients somehow had devised a system to provide fresh air to the King's chamber. An incredible feat! I wondered if the guide was aware of it. If he was, I would think he would have at least mentioned it.

An informal debut of SCARAB was disclosed in a special audience in Cairo late in 1984. Teledyne displayed a 1/4 scale model of the 124RE, with Egyptian Air Force markings, at the Defense Equipment Exhibition at Almaza Air Base. Among those inspecting the model of the new mid-range SCARAB tactical reconnaissance system was Egyptian President Hosni Mubarek, accompanied by Field Marshal Abu Ghazala.

A CASH INFUSION

Back in our hotel, Chuck and I talked about cash flow difficulties at TRA. . We both knew that SCARAB had probably exacerbated the problem, but we didn't know for sure or to what degree. That night in my room, I pulled out the payment schedule from the contract and took a long look. It struck me that in May a $30M payment was due us which, as I recall, was a good six months in the future. I wondered if we could get the payment earlier? It would really be helpful across a number of fronts. One was that while Henry had advanced me the money to add another APACHE assembly station, it still took a long time to pay back $65M!

This was especially true when you consider that we paid it back as APACHE Helicopters were shipped, and our delivery rate at that time was probably around five or six a month. I approached Chuck with my idea the next morning, but he did not think the Egyptians would do it. I decided to give it a try anyway. I had one more trick up my sleeve... remember the agreement I had with Hafez early in the SCARAB Program when the EAF wanted Inertial Navigation Systems, which were not included in our contract?

He still "owed me one."

A HOME RUN!

When I got home, I called Hafez and explained what I had in mind and why it was important to me. Our request went forward. Hafez backed it, and it was approved by the Egyptian Government. We got an early $30M payment! Wow! When the check arrived, our Controller, Arden, burst into my office with a $30M smile! He lavished me with praise, calling me a hero and the best president! Later, he presented me with a framed air-brushed (in color) cash flow document to Corporate reflecting the payment. I had never seen him so pumped!

I'm sure that Henry, sitting In his corner office, was also appreciative of the cash. If I "ruined" one of his quarters, I "made" one for him as well!

Three years later, the first full scale Model 324 Egyptian RPV was displayed at the International Military Equipment Exhibition in Cairo. This time I was there along with Norm Sakamoto, a key engineer and program manager, as well as General Nadim of Sahara Overseas Services.

Norm Sakamoto was a long time employee of TRA and had vast RPV experience. When the SCARAB Program began to develop into a reality, I made Norm the program manager. He was a quiet sort, but enjoyed a good laugh. He was good on his feet and was respected by everyone, friends, colleagues and customers.

FLIGHT TEST

Flight tests began in March 1987 in the desert at Mojave, California, and ran for almost a year. A 44 minute flight on February 28, 1988 was the culmination of four years of dedicated effort by the entire team.

From launch to recovery, it attained all objectives with precision. Completely hands-off, with no man aboard, SCARAB covered a thousand-mile track at Mach 0.8, and returned to a pinpoint recovery area with all the electronic surveillance gear having done its job. Norm was a happy man... and so was I!

The EAF was also pleased. They ordered another 20 SCARABS!

TRA sales reached $200M, with good cash flow and net income.

SCARAB launch with another ready on the Launch - Recovery Vehicle, also showing the Control Module.

THE NECKLACE

A word about General Nadim. He was a slight man, around 5'6" or so and 150 lbs. He had black beady eyes, short salt and pepper hair, and a thin well-groomed pencil mustache. He had been a fighter pilot in the EAF and I could easily picture him peering through a gun sight at some unsuspecting foe, and squeezing the trigger. Nadim had an outgoing personality and gave us studied advice. He and his partner, General Maged were solid citizens as far as we were concerned, and they both enjoyed the respect of the EAF.

I don't recall which trip, but Joan accompanied me to Cairo once. Nadim invited us to join him and his wife, as well as the Mageds, for dinner. Mike Russell, a corporate attorney, was also in Cairo. He was invited, and Chuck may have been there as well. We had a lovely time, and after dinner Nadim pulled out a gift-wrapped package. He gave it to Joan, saying that it was in appreciation for all my efforts on SCARAB. He wanted to thank her especially for putting up with my travels.

She opened the gift to discover a beautiful, intricate silver necklace with large Turquoise stones imbedded in the center piece. Joan was delighted with it and thanked Nadim and his wife.

Back at our hotel, I told her she could not keep the necklace. It was, at minimum, a breach of company protocol/ethics to accept or take gifts from an agent or representative of the company, and could very well be against the law as well. Needless to say, she was disappointed. Wasn't there anything I could do about it? I thought for a moment…

"Yes," I said slowly. "I could do something about it. If Nadim would let me pay for it, you could keep it!" The next day I met with Nadim and thanked him again for the dinner and gift to Joan. I explained to him my moral plight. He couldn't believe that I could not let her keep it.

"It was a gift!" He exclaimed.

He said he gave gifts all the time, it was "what Egyptians do." He also said that he gave gifts to friends, including active military officers, and it was never a problem. I told him that I understood, but it just doesn't work that way in the States. However, *if* he would let me pay for the necklace, Joan could keep it. He relented and told me the cost, shaking his head. I said I would mail him a check as soon as I got home, and I did. Joan was understandably pleased.

DIFFERENT BUSINESS CUSTOMS

Speaking of different business customs around the world, let's take a look at a custom of the Japanese.

As mentioned in Chapter Seven, when I was the General Manager of TRE we had the Yamada Corporation, which was selected by their Navy to negotiate a license for our APN-182 Radar. At Christmas time, Yamada's Los Angeles representative came down to the plant and gave me a bottle of 10-year-old Suntory Scotch, a premier Japanese distillery. It was presented in the classic Japanese fashion of holding out the gift and bowing.

When I was made the President of TRE, I received a bottle of 12-year-old Suntory. When I was president of TRA, I received a bottle of 18-year-old Suntory.

When I was made the President of the Aerospace and Electronics Segment of Teledyne, I was presented with a crystal bottle of 20-year-old Suntory.

One more comment here. When I was in Japan in my corporate role, Yamada took me to a nice dinner in Tokyo, and afterwards, asked me, "Would you like some company for the night?" I declined with thanks, but recognized that this was their custom for esteemed clients. Interesting differences in culture!

THE FAMILY EXPANDS

Howard married Susan Wilson in 1988 and they settled in the San Fernando Valley. Susan graduated from USC, and Howard from the University of California at Santa Barbara. Later, he earned his MBA at Pepperdine University. He went to work for Susan's father in his Cadillac Agency, Casa de Cadillac in Sherman Oaks. Over the years, Howard expanded the business to include additional automobile franchises.

They have two lovely daughters, Hanna, born in 1991, and Madeline, in 1993. The girls graduated from Cornell and SMU respectively, and have joined their dad in the business.

The family on vacation at the La Jolla Beach and Tennis Club Hotel-mid-1990's (left to right, back row: Howard, Susan, Paul, Joan and me; front row: Hanna, Madeline and Cameron)

GLOBAL HAWK

There was one more project of high interest that appeared prior to my departure for the Corporate Offices. The Defense Advanced Research Projects Agency (DARPA), which does classified cutting-edge research for the DoD, put a project out for bid, which we won. It was a "Proof of Concept" contract for a high altitude Intelligence, Surveillance and Reconaissance (ISR) RPV, which ultimately became the Global Hawk. It is now flying missions around the clock in Iraq and Afghanistan. Bob Mitchell, who replaced me at TRA, graciously calls me "the father of Global Hawk." I was there at the beginning, but Bob did the heavy lifting.

Wherever Global Hawk is in the world, it is in direct contact with our satellites. At the other end of the satellite(s), is a U.S. team flying it. These missions are typically flown out of Beale Air Force base in Northern California.

U.S. Air Force GLOBAL Hawk on the runway, 1988

Its mission, as noted above is ISR; it is not a weapon carrier. It flies at 60,000' and can stay up for 24 hours, day/night. To give you an idea of how capable this aircraft is, it can photograph an area the size of the state of Illinois, from altitude, in 24 hours, and with a resolution of 3 feet! Global Hawk accommodates a variety of payloads. For example, long range electro-optical/infra-red sensors. The aircraft has added a new dimension to persistent airborne surveillance, with no pilot at risk.

Models of TRA products, 1988

ANOTHER SURPRISE

In early 1988, Bill Rutherford called and asked me to come and see him in his office. I sat down and he told me that George wanted to see me.

"OK, do you know what it's about?" I said.

He thought about it for a moment and then said, "He wants to talk about your future."

"Really?" I was puzzled.

The next morning, I flew up to the Santa Monica Airport and drove over to the office. George was alone, and after I came in he closed the door. He said that he and Henry were going to re-organize Teledyne, and they wanted me to head up the Aerospace and Electronics part! Oh my!

REFLECTIONS

After my meeting with George at the Corporate Office about the reorganization of Teledyne, and my new role in it, I sat down at home and reflected on my 12 years running TRE, and four years running TRA. They were amazing years, but very different experiences.

In 1972, TRE was my move back into electronics and a general manager position, following four years in Washington, D.C. The company had successfully designed and built both the Landing Radars for the APOLLO Mission to the Moon, and the VIKING Mission to Mars. What it hadn't done, was build much of a history in consistent, recurring product manufacturing, leading to contin-ued profitable sales growth and an improved, competitive line of products and customers. There was a lot of undeveloped talent there as well.

During my time at TRE, we developed the Computer Display Unit, taking us from "black box" sub-systems into navigation systems, and expanding our customer base with new solid state technology, including Planar Array Antennas. We won major contracts which provided a continuous "feed" of new technology and customers such as the U.S. Air Force, Germany, Japan and China. We kept our Navy customer, and moved our third generation of Doppler Radar, the APN-217, into fleet aircraft.

The leadership across the disciplines grew exponentially with the company, and our expanding resources accommodated improvements in manufacturing capital equipment, engineering R&D and facility upgrades, a much needed effort! We had consistent momentum, much of it provided by multi-year year contracts, which led to our establishment as a separate Teledyne Company. I don't think many folks, if any, ever thought TRE would be separated from "big brother," TRA. But, on May 12, 1980, Hello! TRE never looked back and continued to develop people, products and growth. It was a very special time for me.

TRA was a different story. Its "heyday" supplying RPV's in support of our forces in Vietnam had ended. It was running on its target business, augmented by some sub contract work. Until, of course, it got the contract from Hughes Helicopter to build two prototype APACHE Attack Helicopter Airframes. The Hughes/Ryan Team went on to win the production contract from the Army, and TRA had a new life.

I don't know if TRA ever had such a demanding production contract as it did with the APACHE. The company learned the difference between traditional aircraft machining and dealing with composite technologies. The transition from building prototypes to building production airframes across a number of stations, at a growing rate per month, was a huge challenge. Establishing an assembly line supported by a substantial machine shop and numerous subcontractors, hiring and training employees, and gearing up for steadily increasing production rates was an urgent and demanding requirement. The company struggled mightily, but couldn't gain traction in making the required delivery schedule.

The company president was fired, and for reasons unknown to me, I was brought from TRE to fill the breech. Looking back, I wonder what in the world Teledyne management was thinking, to offer me the presidency. Better yet, what in the world was I thinking to accept it! The problems at TRA were a world away from those I encountered at TRE. Even the scale was daunting!

If nothing else, I brought a positive, "let's get It done" attitude, a love of the manufacturing process, and a willingness to learn. As I worked (literally around the clock) to get a grip on the company and the APACHE problems, I can honestly say that there were times I was scared to death that I would not be able to find the solution before my time ran out with Teledyne management, or, that Hughes/U.S. Army would cancel us for breach of contract-non delivery.

Certainly, winning a multi-year order from the Navy for FIREBEE Targets early in my tenure helped my self-confidence. But, I also wondered where was my marketing team?

As you have read, I reached out for help...and got it. Not only from McDonnel Douglas, but from Henry Singleton. His financial contribution gave me the money to duplicate the Center Mate Station that solved the production problem and set us up for success.

APACHE was probably the key in Teledyne's decision to bring me up to Corporate. Certainly my success at TRE contributed, as well as FIREBEE, SCARAB, and the beginning of GLOBAL HAWK. But, in my opinion, the scale of the APACHE Attack Helicopter Program produced the cash and profit that sold Henry on me.

I left TRA in the same state that I left TRE: successful, growing companies with sound managements and healthy financials. I couldn't have asked for more.

CHAPTER NINE

Teledyne Corporate: 1988-1997

"In the old days, I would walk out in the plant and look for problems. In my Corporate job, I didn't have to do that, all I had to do was wait for the phone to ring."

George explained in some detail what he and Henry had in mind. It was a major change in Teledyne's design and thought process! Typically, they would buy a company that fit their business model and would keep the owner or president on to run it as a Teledyne Company. Over the years, Henry and George had gathered up some 120 companies under the Teledyne banner. The time had come to integrate the companies into a more classic organizational structure. What initially began as two segments, Aerospace and Electronics, and Metals and Manufacturing, ultimately became three segments: Aerospace and Electronics (A&E), Specialty Metals (SM), and Consumer and Indusrial (CI). I would be responsible for A&E, the largest segment.

This involved more than just the few people chosen to run these segments. Teledyne had been operating for years in the "George and Henry" mode of doing business, with a substantial number of accountants, lawyers, and staff looking after the operations of the various companies. This "corporate staff" (including a cadre of some 20 group executives), was not necessarily thrilled with the change, many of them liked the good old ways, and were in no hurry to help the newly appointed leadership. In many cases, they were now "farther from the throne" since there were suddenly interlopers between them and Henry and George.

GETTING ORGANIZED

Initially, I was a Teledyne Vice President, as was Bill Rutledge. We were rapidly made Sr. Vice Presidents and then, when Henry and George actually launched the new organization, we were made Segment Presidents. I was Segment President for A&E and Bill for SM.

All of this happened in a matter of a few months. I think there was a reason for that rapid promotion sequence. George told me that he had asked Bill Rutherford to let me come up to Corporate for months, but, Bill kept saying "No." He told George that while I had solved the APACHE problem, re-started the FIREBEE Target line, and had the SCARAB program on track, I had not yet come up with my replacement at TRA. I could hardly believe it! Bill never talked to me about a replacement, never! If he had, I would have been on the phone to a head-hunter in a flash.

Meanwhile, Bill Rutledge was in a holding pattern at the Latrobe Office until George could break me loose. When he finally got Rutherford to let me go, he was behind schedule, so George moved everything up when he had both of us free. I think that's what happened.

Bill, was hired in 1986, as the Eastern Group Executive. He was responsible for Teledyne's Specialty Metals companies from his office in Latrobe, Pennsylvania. This was the home of the Vasco metals company, which George had started, and would become Teledyne Vasco and Teledyne Allvac when he joined forces with Henry. Prior to that, Bill had been involved as a general manager in the FMC Company, and the division that made the Bradley Fighting Vehicle. He held a degree in Metallurgy from Lafayette College and a Master's in Finance from George Washington University. I met him when we both came to corporate.

George never told me why I was selected as the head of A&E. There were a number of capable company presidents in A&E. We all knew that Henry had strong friendships with his group executives, especially Allen Orbuch in the Systems Group, Bill Rutherford in the Pacific Group, and Marv Blitz in the Precision Group. Other than seeing Henry at Profit Plan meetings, and of course our few private sessions, I did not know the man well.

Over the 16 years I ran my two Teledyne Companies, I spent much more time with George as Teledyne's Chief Operating Officer. We got along well, and as noted earlier, he sponsored my membership in Conquistadores. We enjoyed great times together at their meetings! George had to be the man who had favored me for the top A&E job, but Henry always had the final say.

CHARTING A NEW COURSE

I am sure you have noticed by now, that this is a different format than the two previous chapters. It is a major difference because this new job is a whole different thing.

My previous life was devoted to companies that developed and produced products. I worried about having enough non-recurring engineering to support our technical staff, and enough manufacturing to support our production lines. I worried about new business, competition, technology, unions, defense and congressional budgets, and meeting my profit plan numbers. At corporate I no longer did any of that. Instead, I was running an organization of leaders.

I was removed from the "nitty gritty" of day-to-day company business. Instead, I managed leaders who ran companies, and group executives who ran groups of companies. This was a major change for me! I was now disassociated from my previous life of 16 years as a line company president. I enjoyed and grew from the experience I gained in those years, and perhaps that was why I was here?

I was thoroughly surprised with the company re-organization and my promotion, of which I was very proud. I had always aspired to being a company president, and now, I was a segment president, in charge of many companies, thousands of employees, and hundreds of millions of dollars of business, but in a different setting and under different circumstances and rules.

EARLY CHALLENGE

Under the new set-up, I was responsible for 41 companies. An early challenge was sorting them out. I needed to look at their businesses, technologies, sales, income, and products to determine whether to combine them with another company, sell them, or keep them as a stand-alone company. When I asked George about a staff, he made available a young corporate accountant named Dave Oliver. All due respect to Dave, that just wasn't much to work with given the magnitude of the task at hand! But, we set to work.

A very important item was getting our Segment financials organized per Teledyne policy for reporting purposes. This took time, given the limited manpower and number of companies involved. I was also trying to at least talk with my company presidents by phone, most of whom I did not know, nor did I know their company. It was an arduous task. I might even categorize it as a "Herculean task."

SPEAKING UP

Perhaps six months or so had gone by when George said he "thought I was slow getting on top of my companies." That was the closest to a criticism I ever got from George. I was working as hard and fast as I could, as was Dave. His comment hurt my feelings, the inference being that Bill Rutledge was doing a better job than I was. I did not respond to it at the time because I felt it would be defensive in nature, and therefore inappropriate.

Still, his comment rankled me every time I thought of it, because I thought it unfair. A year or so later, I had a good opportunity to bring it up while we were bunking together at a Conquistadores Ranch Meeting in Wyoming.

The gist of what I said was, "I don't know if you recall saying to me a while after the re-organization announcement that you thought I was slow getting on top of my companies? I thought that unfair. Let me tell you why.

I only had Dave Oliver and a secretary to integrate all the financials on my new companies for reporting purposes. Not to mention deciding how to organize them, which depended on their size, products, facilities, technologies and so on, of which I knew very little. This was difficult compared with the segment that Bill was running in the form of the Eastern Group/Specialty Metals, which existed *before* the re-organization. This allowed them to enjoy an existing office and staff of 14 in Latrobe. When assigned one or two more companies in the re-orgaization, it was no big deal to bring them into the homgenous fold of Metals Companies where all their financials, profit plans etc. would be smoothly processed by the staff for the Corporate Office.

A&E, on the other hand, was made up of a "dog's breakfast" of 41 disparate companies. From high tech electronics and software, to general aviation engines and diesel tank engines, down to components like relays and hybrid circuits. Our companies spanned batteries, helicopter fuselages, traveling wave tubes, radars, computers, inertial navigation systems, and on and on, across a myriad of technologies and expertise…all manned by Dave and I."

I stopped talking. I had gotten it off my chest, and felt much better. George sat stunned for a minute, and then simply said, "I had no idea." The subject never came up again.

RELOCATING

High on my to-do list was to find a new home. When George promoted me, it was on condition that I move to Century City or close by. Joan and I started our search. In the late 1980s Century City's real estate market was very tight. It was primarily an area of condos, which was what we were looking for. There was a nice development near the office called Century Park which we liked, but nothing was for sale there. I even offered a potential seller a $25,000 bonus if he would sell me his condo. He said he couldn't find any place to go!

We finally found an upscale place in Century Woods, just a few blocks from the office in a gated, wooded community of condos and town homes. Carol Burnett had a town home there, and it was an easy walk to the office as well. We bought a first floor unit with two bedrooms and two baths. It had lovely distressed wood floors, a dining room, and a big living room with exposed overhead beams and a big fireplace. The master bedroom also had a fireplace. There were two covered porches as well as two parking places beneath the building. In a tight market we paid $900,000 for it, but when we sold our home it would knock the loan down quite a bit. Timing is everything!

Joan understood the deal about moving to Century City, but her heart was not in it. She had periodic spells with cancer, which her oncology team always managed to get under control. But her roots and social circle were in Rancho Bernardo, and she didn't want to leave. Basically, what ended up happening was that I flew up to the Santa Monica Airport in the company King Air from TRA on Monday mornings, and home the same way on Friday night. Initially, Joan drove up to spend several days and nights at the condo each week, and we would have fun at local bistros and restaurants. Jimmy's was a favorite place of hers. I was hopeful that she would come up permanently, but she never did. Over time she came less and less as her health slowly deteriorated.

GOING GLOBAL

George was just full of surprises. He called me into his office one day and told me he also wanted me to be responsible for all of Teledyne's Corporate International Offices (CIOs). There were 17 of them scattered around the globe. CIOs were organized to assist our companies in the marketing and sales of their products in foreign markets. I suppose George thought I would be good at helping in that area, what with my international experience.

CIO sales ran about $500M a year and were headed by two men: Leo Killen and Will Strong.

LEO KILLEN

Leo Killen, whom I knew well, managed the CIOs in Belgium, Italy, France, Germany, Spain, U.K., Israel, and Saudi Arabia from his Geneva office. His CIOs were mostly robust, but several were marginal. We closed the Spain and Italy offices at some point in time. Leo was an excellent manager and his CIOs reflected it.

PAST IS PROLOGUE

As you may recall, Leo was my boss at North American Aviation's Autonetics Division. The Autonetics field representative for the southwest region was a fellow named Gene Meng, based in Oklahoma City, Oklahoma. I was presenting a proposal and giving a briefing to the General Dynamics Fort Worth Division. I had never met Gene, but he was taking me to the meeting. He told me to meet him at his motel, and since I was arriving late I could stay with him.

I arrived at the motel around midnight and went to his room. The motel was organized in sort of a bungalow fashion. His door was a step or two up from the ground. I knocked on the door and waited. I was about to knock again, when the door flew open. I looked up and saw this large man (Gene was 6'5") standing in the doorway, totally nude!

I said, "Gene?"

He said, "Yeah, come on in. I have company so you'll have to sleep on the couch."

When I awoke in the morning, his "company" had left, and we made our trip to Fort Worth.

Well, guess who Leo had hired as our Belgium CIO in Brussels? Yep, old Gene Meng himself! He and I met up later in Europe, and he was very apologetic about his behavior. He was married at the time too. When I was put in charge of all the CIOs, I'll bet Gene had some concerns!

He said, "I hope you won't hold it against me..."

I laughed and said, "No problem, but it's a small world, 'eh Gene?"

The story tells you that you never know who or in what circumstance you're going to run into someone from the past...good or bad! There's a life lesson here.

WILL STRONG

Will Strong managed his CIOs from Century City, but he traveled a great deal. The CIOs were in Argentina, Venezuela, Australia, Hong

Kong, Japan, South Korea, Taiwan, and Mexico. Will was a longtime Teledyne employee, and had reported to George, as had Leo. His Tokyo office was significant, not only in terms of sales, but also because they actively assisted our companies in expanding product sales in-country. That office was headed up by Peter Katsuno. Peter had actually established a "trading company" there which did business in its own name, and enjoyed sales in the range of $50M a year.

I had several meetings with Will and was not impressed, despite his qualifications. He was a graduate of the Thunderbird International School in Arizona with good Spanish skills. I wanted to see how his CIOs stood up in terms of sales, companies using them, information on the local manager running the office, and the basic questions: are you really helping companies sell, and are you giving us a return on investment?

Will was very defensive, and obviously not used to someone questioning what he was doing with his CIOs. George had more important things to worry about than finding out what Will was or wasn't doing. After just a few months of working for me, Will took an international sales positon with one of our companies, Teledyne Allvac, an SM company located in South Carolina. Godspeed!

I took a fast trip to the Far East and called on each CIO. Several of the CIO mangers were suspect, as was the value of some offices. For example, I found a fellow named Jim Smith who worked for Will out of Honolulu, Hawaii. I phoned Jim and asked what he did, and why he was in Hawaii... He told me he was much closer to the Far East offices, for which he says he was responsible, than he would be in Los Angeles. I agreed, but said that he was an awfully long way from everyone else. Close the office! I will come back and talk some more about the Far East CIOs.

TERRY LYONS

As one would hope, things got better at A&E over time. One of the reasons for this improvement was my hire of a bright, young accountant from Teledyne Crittenden. Terry Lyons was a University of Cincinnati accounting graduate. Terry and I shared a similar sense of humor and outlook on life. He was wise beyond his years and often pointed out things that I had missed. He had a good grasp of "how things worked at Corporate" and was a huge benefit to me both professionally and personally.

He was a perfect example of what I was talking about in the chapter on TRE relating to encouraging young talent. Terry blossomed under conditions that provided for his growth and development as an executive.

MORE FAMILY EXPANSION

Paul married Sylvaine Alsis in 1990 in San Diego. Paul had a condominium in Escondido, and that's where they resided. He went into the painting business and in 1991, their son Cameron was born. Cameron is now working in the commercial electrical business in and around San Diego. Unfortunately, the marriage was unsuccessful.

PARIS AIR SHOW
SALON INTERNATIONAL de l'AERONAUTIQUE
et de l'ESPACE

Launched in 1909, the biggest event in aerospace exhibition is the Paris Air Show at Le Bourget airport. All the "big boys" are there:

Boeing, Lockheed, Northrop-Grumman, Rolls Royce, GE, Airbus, British Air, Lufthansa, American, and others.

Virtually all of my companies participate in the Paris show. I play a sponsoring role and Berkley Baker, a long time Teledyne organizer, is also involved. Typically, we buy a "Chalet" which is made up of two double wide trailers set up with a kitchen, rest rooms, bar/restaurant, private conference rooms, and an outdoor area with tables and chairs. The location and view of the runways from the Chalet is important so your guests can enjoy the take-offs and landings of the flight demonstrations.

The cost of the show runs about $2M and is allocated to the participating companies.

Not only do our companies show their own products and systems, but they also turn out to support their customers' programs, such as the McDonnell Douglas Corporation with an APACHE Helicopter at the show. They're also there to support flying demonstrations.

Above and beyond commercial aircraft, my A&E companies provide a host of systems and subsystems to fighter aircraft such as the F-16, F-18 and many others. Plus, of course, supporting Primes and their customers. The show is a lot of work but also very enjoyable. Watching the flying demonstrations right over your head is impressive (and deafening)! Walking through the static exhibit area is also worthwhile.

THE VOYAGER

I was particularly proud of one of my companies, Teledyne Continental Motors, a major producer of general aviation engines.

The Voyager aircraft was featured at the air show in a special exhibit. You may recall that in 1986, the Voyager flew a record breaking, non-stop circumnavigation of the earth. It flew 216 hours, covering 26,178 miles! Amazing!

Continental designed and built the two liquid-cooled, 110 horse power engines that powered that flight. One was in the nose of the aircraft and the other was in the rear, in a pusher configuration. Only one was used at a time to conserve fuel. The only time the aircraft needed both engines at the same time was for take-off.

I was thrilled to be a guest at the Smithsonian Air and Space Museum in Washington, D.C. for the induction of the Voyager (both aircraft and an exact replica of our engine) as a permanent exhibit. It was a spectacular event.

As you can imagine, Paris is packed for this event! Reservations for the top hotels (The Ritz, Crillon, Meurice etc.) have to be made at least a year in advance. Joan's and my favorite hotel is the Crillon. It is situated for beautiful views of the Place de la Concorde, the Tuileries, and Napoleon's Obelisk in the center of the Place. During World War II the German Luftwaffe Headquarters were located there.

Today, the American Embassy is just across the avenue. When I was in the Commerce Department we often visited the Embassy because it had a large Post Exchange in the basement. The French wines there were first rate and reasonably priced. Bringing home French wine was easy with a Diplomatic Passport!

LE TOUR de' ARGENT

Another treat is dinner at one of Paris' many fine restaurants. The bookings for the top restaurants are also highly sought after and very expensive. There is a very famous one, right across the street from the famed Cathedral de' Notre Dame, called Le Tour de' Argent. It has a magnificent view of the cathedral, especially at night when it is all lit up. The restaurant specializes in roast duck, with a lovely presentation of the duck before it is carved at your table. Delicious, but pricey.

Joan and I were there one night as guests of Rolls Royce. We were enjoying a nice glass of burgundy when I saw some familiar faces entering the dining room. They were seated right by the big picture window with the best view of Notre Dame. It was Jeff Amacker, the President of Teledyne Controls, which happened to be one of my companies. He was accompanied by his wife, his marketing VP and his wife, plus four other Controls people ...and one guest! Eight Controls people and one guest, ridiculous!

Jeff saw me and knew he was out of line. It was a horrible abuse of privilege, let alone the cost. He found me the next day at our Chalet to apologize. I told him I was disappointed, and that he should be very careful with his and his employees' expense accounts for that dinner. Need I say more?

Israeli Prime Minister Rabin was on our floor at the Crillon one year, and we ran into him and his security team at the elevator. We exchanged morning greetings, but when the elevator came, security made sure no one else got on it. I think that was the same year he was assassinated.

RETIREMENT

In 1989 there were two notable retirements. After 29 years with his company, Henry decided to call it quits. Few knew it at the time, but Henry was suffering from brain cancer. The other retirement was Bill Rutherford's. George told me one day to inform Bill that he was to retire.

I said something like, "You mean you want *me* to tell him?"

George said, "Yes, he works for you."

So one day, on my way to Corporate, I stopped in to see Bill in his office. I told him what George had said, and asked what kind of retirement party he would like. Bill really had nothing to say. Honestly, neither did I.

While we're on the subject, George also told me to tell Leo Killen that he was to retire, because Leo worked for me too. When I was in Geneva the next time, I sat down with him and gave him the news. It was hard for me. He was surprised and disappointed. He had no plans to retire, but he did so anyways. Given their years of friendship, I would have thought that George would have wanted to speak with both of them himself.

CIO INITIATIVES

In the 1990s, with my CIO hat on, I planned three special technical exhibits for interested Teledyne Companies: one in Tokyo, one in Milan, and one in Moscow. Most companies wanted to participate. The appropriate CIOs went to work organizing, and did a splendid job.

The exhibits were held over a two-day period. I kicked them off as the lead speaker at the gala dinner the night before the exhibit opened. Each one of the exhibits had its own story, but let me tell you about preparations for Tokyo, which was our first foreign exhibit. I wanted to open the dinner with a welcoming speech to our (many) Japanese guests, *in Japanese*.

I found a Japanese lady at the Corporate Office and asked her if she would translate my speech into Japanese, phonetically? She agreed, and worked through my speech. I spent hours working on pronunciation and getting it to where I was comfortable with it.

When Joan and I arrived in Japan, Peter Katsuno met us at the airport. Even before we left the airport he wanted to hear my speech! He knew, of course, that I planned to give it in Japanese. We sat down at a nearby bench.

I said, "Listen, Peter, I have slaved over this speech for weeks, practicing it. Correct my pronunciation, but do not change the speech."

I began reading it to him. After about four sentences he interrupted me, "No, no, Hudson, that is not Japanese, that is Los Angeles Japanese! It would not be well received at all here in Tokyo. Give it to me and I will fix it." Peter changed about 30 percent of it, but I could handle the changes.

The night before the gala dinner in Tokyo, Joan and I joined Trudy and Bill Rutledge for drinks at our hotel. Bill wanted to take the subway to the exhibit hall where the dinner was to be held, and I couldn't talk him out of it.

A POOR DECISION

The night of the dinner, the ladies decided to go in a limo (like I should have) while Bill and I struck off for the subway station. He was in charge and proceeded to get us very lost in a very short time. Fortunately, we found a man who spoke English. He pointed us toward the right train and showed us how to get on it.

In the meantime, I was sweating bullets because I was the lead speaker and we were going to be late. We arrived, finally, running most of the way to the hall. I was out of breath and sweating. I got to the rostrum just after our Ambassador Mike Armacost finished his speech, also in Japanese. Mike was a classmate in the White House Fellows with me. He received a Ph.D. from Stanford. After his fellowship year and a few years at State, he was appointed Undersecretary of State for Political Affairs. Following that, he became the Ambassador to Japan. He kindly accepted my request that he support our Technical Exhibit by agreeing to speak. He and his wife, Bonnie are good people.

My speech was a hit, the Japanese loved the thoughtfulness and gave me a big hand. The show was superb as well.

Since I gave my speeches in every country's native language, I always had it checked by a local for language variations. Great save, Peter! Thanks! Another lesson here.

AN OPTION OPENS

In early 1989, I received a phone call from Barry Shillito, who was on the board of the Thiokol Corporation. Barry, you recall, was the President of Teledyne Ryan Aeronautical when I ran Teledyne Ryan

Electronics in the early '70s. Thiokol designed and manufactured solid propellant rocket engines for the space program among other products. Neil Armstrong, famed Apollo 11 astronaut and a fellow Conquistador, was also on the Board.

Barry said the company, headquartered in Ogden, Utah, was looking for a new CEO. Would I be interested? We talked about it for a while and I agreed to meeting with them. It was arranged, and I flew up to Ogden.

The headquarters was located in the hills/mountains among big pine trees outside of town. It was rustic, but attractive. Not to mention comfortable and well equipped, I liked it. I met the board, and it was nice to have two friends on it, Barry and Neil. The others were very solicitous.

They asked questions relating to my background, interests, and desires. I asked my questions as well. All in all, it was a comfortable meeting. I knew they liked me, and I liked them. I had always wanted to be the CEO of a New York Stock Exchange company. Teledyne was one, and Thiokol was another! I told them I would think about it and let them know. When I left, Barry told me that they did have another candidate.

No doubt I was interested, but in thinking about it, I also thought I had a shot at being CEO of Teledyne. After 20 some years it knew me, and I knew it. I sat down with Joan and we talked about making a change. Until I was ready to declare serious interest, she was non-committal.

Several days later, the HR vice president from Thiokol called me to follow-up on my interest, and to invite me to visit them again. This time he suggested I bring my wife. He named a date that worked for the board. "Fine, let me talk with Joan and get back to you." I said. I told Joan about the invitation and the date. She said she had a tax problem with the apartments. After selling the grove, we bought a 20-unit apartment complex in Pacific Beach, and Joan ran it. She was meeting with the CPA on that date.

I said, "Well, OK, but surely you can change it."

"No, I can't."

WON'T GO

The bottom line was that she refused to go to the meeting. She wouldn't move to Ogden either! I told her the company had a nice jet, and if all else failed, I could commute much like I had from Century City. I suggested she could fly back to Rancho Bernardo whenever she felt like it.

"No, nothing doing. I won't go, period." She was adamant.

To some extent, I can understand Joan's thought process. Her longtime and trusted oncology team was local, as was Paul. Howard and family were relatively close, as was Cameron. Her friends of many years lived close by as well. Moving away, even with private air transportation, would be hard on her. Frankly, I think her experience in Washington, D.C. soured her on making any job change that required moving, whether to Century City or Ogden.

Obviously, if my wife wouldn't go to meet the board I was finished as a candidate. I was upset with her to say the least. However, I called the Thiokol HR VP and explained as best I could that we couldn't come. He pleaded with me to come. *I was the only candidate the board was inviting back*. I said I was really sorry and thanked them for considering me. Adding insult to injury, less than two years later Goodrich Aerospace bought Thiokol. They were more than generous with the executives, financially!

I considered telling George that I had been contacted by Thiokol regarding their CEO position. I thought it would be a good opportunity to ask him what, if any, plans Teledyne had for me in the future? On the other hand, since Joan had "scotched" the promotion, I didn't feel comfortable relating the approach by Thiokol to George when I had already turned it down.

You could argue it either way, but I decided not to bring it up.

STORM CLOUDS

I want to stop here and go back to the late 1980s. As I mentioned earlier, this book is about what was important in my life, and many of the people and things that influenced it. My career at Teledyne, of course, was a big part of it. The last nine years were spent at the Corporate Office. The events and people there had an especially big impact on me and my companies.

While I was busy at TRA in 1988, enjoying myself building and delivering production hardware, many of the problems I would have to deal with later at Corporate were "already in the oven" at other Teledyne Companies.

As It turns out, my appointment to Century City in mid-1988 was the zenith of my career, although I didn't know it at the time! For a good part of the following years, I was scrambling to deal with losses in a number of my companies. From fixed price development contracts and dealing with lawsuits against other of my companies, which were being pursued by the government, issues abounded. Among my headaches were the "Whistle Blower" Suits.

So, what happened in the late '80s?

The fall of the Berlin Wall signaled the end of the Cold War and the end of the Reagan defense budgets, which did indeed contract under both Presidents Bush and Clinton's direction. A smaller defense budget meant less business and more competition for contract awards.

Also in that timeframe, Congress updated a Civil War Era Statute known as the "False Claims Act." This act, along with companion legislation such as the Truth in Negotiation Act, significantly changed the rules and balance of power between the government and defense contractors. This added to the already Byzantine world of government contracting. In some cases, customer/supplier matters which had heretofore been considered purely "administrative," became criminalized.

The False Claims Act was interpreted as essentially a "Bounty Hunter" statute. It provided substantial financial incentives to employees, encouraging them to take their concerns about business practices to the government, rather than to management. "Whistle Blowers" were told by the government that they would get 15-30% of any recovered funds from the accused companies. This is certainly not to excuse bad behavior by my companies, or any companies for that matter, but it also "might" encourage the filing of unsubstantiated charges. One example was that Teledyne paid a fine of $2.1M to settle a suit without admitting wrongdoing. The employee who made the accusation received $430,000 from that amount. (This refers to Qui Tam suits).

Adding to this perfect storm was the Pentagon's policy shift in favor of competitive fixed-price *development* contracts in lieu of cost-type development contracts. Cost-type development contracts had been in use since the 1970s for complex new defense systems such as aircraft, ships, and missiles. The net effect of all the changes was to significantly shift the financial risk from the government to its suppliers[4]

Teledyne would experience great pain and substantial financial loss, due in large part to these changes in the political landscape. Managing the collateral effects took a tremendous toll, costing jobs and careers. It was professionally and personally difficult for me.

Teledyne Electronics, located in Southern California, was the first to run into trouble in 1988. It was suspended by the Defense Logistics Agency because one of the company's consultants allegedly payed a bribe to obtain business. The scandal that TE was caught up in, involved other big defense industry companies as well, and came to be known as "Operation Ill Wind." I will use the term Ill Wind to describe the overall environment of our government contracting troubles.

Another was Teledyne Systems, which was accused of "over-charging" the government. The third was Teledyne Relays for "improper testing procedures." The Relays charge flies in the face of the extraordinary field reliability of the company's relays, which supplied over 50% of its popular TO-5 Relays for years

---

4   This is a very large subject, and this is not the place to pursue it in detail. If you are interested in learning more, please see my Harvard Business Review article, referenced in Chapter 2, p. 39. The article points out the fundamental flaws of imposing fixed price type contracts on cutting edge development contracts and the detrimental effects on both the government and suppliers

to industry and the military. Quality is not "tested" into the product, it is "designed" in. Hence, the government's charge that there were improprieties in testing procedure may carry the day in a court, but it won't convince the thousands of happy users otherwise.

While the government claimed hundreds of millions of dollars in damages, the Systems and Relays issues were settled for $100M. "Whistle Blowers" were involved in both cases.

Once an issue was raised, Teledyne had outside lawyers who descended on the offending company. There was little I could do regarding operations or the legal proceedings. Lawyers were now running the show. The "Ill Wind" period cast a long shadow over Teledyne, and me.

A NEW CEO

At the 1990 Paris Air Show, George called me over to a private table. He told me that the board had decided to make Bill Rutledge the CEO! That was a shocker. George went on to say that I should immediately announce it to all our people here. Although the timing would never be "good" for me to announce it to my executives at the air show, it was really hard. I couldn't imagine why he would choose that time and place.

Still, I made the announcement.

Since the companies having difficulty reported to me, even though I'd served for such a short time in my new position, I was responsible for their actions. I could not legitimately argue with the decision to promote Bill. Understandably, the board did not think it could promote me, even if it wanted to.

Bill's former segment was divided in two, with Gordon Bean named to run the Metals companies, and Gary Riley, the Consumer and Industrial companies.

If I had had any inkling of Bill's coming promotion, I would have probably taken the Thiokol position. The timing was so close, a margin of just five or six months! I may be wrong, but I think under those circumstances Joan may have agreed to go to Ogden. Again, I don't know and never will.

THE AFFAIR

Now, for an interesting corporate-type item. I was at my desk one day when the phone rang. Sharon must have been out of the office since it kept ringing. I answered the call. A woman was on the line, and she was in a high state of anxiety. I could hardly understand what she was saying. When she stopped for a breath, I asked her who she was and the reason for the call. She settled down and told me her name. She was calling to tell me about one of my executives, a Group Executive, yet!.

I said, "What about him?"

She told me that they had been in a long-term relationship, and it seemed that he would not leave his wife. She was angry, and said she had irrefutable evidence that he was writing-off their relationship on Teledyne's dime! She had receipts for numerous expenses incurred by her, her son, and her mother, that she knew he had put on his expense account.

What's the old saying about a woman scorned?

I was shocked. He and his wife were church-going people and I could not imagine him involved in such a tawdry thing. I asked her to send me the receipts and any information that would assist us in determining the facts of the matter. She did and we did. He was "cooked."

I called, and asked him to come and see me, since he was reasonably close. I had Rich Harshman, our Ethics Officer, Dan Lukasik, our HR person, and maybe a lawyer, I don't recall, in my office. I explained to him why we were having this meeting, and what we had found. His first words were, "I'm dead." I don't know what happened at his home, but he was done at Teledyne.

THE GREAT 8

By the mid-90s, we had fashioned A&E into eight companies: Allvac (titanium products) and Wah Chang (exotic metals) the others were, Brown (software), Aircraft Products (general aviation engines), General Products (military and commercial specialty trucks) Ryan Aeronautical (targets, helicopters and unmanned air vehicles), Micro-electronics (hybrid circuits) and Controls, (collision avoidance systems for commercial airlines). Excluding CIO sales, A&E generated sales of $1.5B.

1993 held a surprise for me. Don Rice, an old friend of George's, was announced as our new President and Chief Operating Officer (COO). I walked over to Bill's office and asked, "Why not me?"

He hardly looked up from his desk as he said, "It was a board decision."

"Please don't leave the company." He followed up. Understandably, I was disappointed. It also would have been thoughtful if I had been given a "heads up" before the announcement! Years later, I asked our (then) general counsel why she thought Don was brought aboard. She said, "It was *because* of the Ill Wind issue."

I worked a great deal with Don, and found him to be pleasant when he wanted to be, but an autocrat most of the time. He was tough on both employees and executives at any level. Fortunately, he and I got along, though we came from vastly different backgrounds. Don was very accomplished. He had a Ph.D., was CEO of the Rand Corporation (a Think Tank), and served as Secretary of the Air Force.

But, Don had never run a manufacturing company, which stood at the heart of Teledyne. He'd never worried about developing a new product, labor issues, or the delicate balance of engineering and manufacturing needs. He had never developed and lived with a Profit Plan.

As if we didn't have enough problems, Teledyne soon became the target of a "Hostile Takeover" by a company named WHX, and its president, Ron LaBow. Teledyne put in a big and extended effort to thwart WHX. The attempt was aimed at the approximate amount of overfunding in Teledyne's pension plan. While the takeover ultimately failed, LaBow became a significant Teledyne shareholder in the process, and got a seat on the board.

BAD NEWS FROM ASIA

I said earlier in this chapter, that I would return to our CIOs in the Far East. Two things transpired that resulted in the closing of both our Seoul and Hong Kong offices. While overseas Jim Riddle, our manager in Seoul, had a massive stroke and was completely stricken. He couldn't walk or talk following the incident. His wife was Taiwanese, and spoke broken English at best.

The message I got from Seoul advised that Jim had cancelled his insurance just before all this and his wife had no money to take Jim, their children, and their belongings to live with his parents in Pennsylvania. Would Teledyne pick up the bill for moving them? Without addressing all I could say about Jim, and this most unfortunate situation, I said we would pay for their move. I just couldn't refuse them under the circumstances and still sleep at night.

Alfred Choy, our Hong Kong manager, had a much different problem. He was cheating on his expense account and an internal audit caught it. Alfred was a nice young man, and enjoyed his work with Teledyne. I called, and asked him what in the world he was thinking? He told me that in his circle, if you did not have a car you were "nothing." Even though the entire island only had 22 miles of roads, that was their attitude.

The only way he thought he could accomplish getting a car was "padding" his expense account. What a shame!

CONNECTING

I liked to stay in contact with my companies. On a fairly regular basis I would take Terry, and perhaps others depending on the circumstances, for a swing through my companies. For example, we would fly commercially to Atlanta, and have a company Citation ll pick us up. From there we'd fly to a company location, such as Aircraft Products in Mobile, Alabama.

We would have drinks and dinner with the company president and his senior staff, and in the morning, tour the factory. Usually, we'd also get a briefing on the company's Profit Plan status. In the late afternoon, we would fly to the next company, such as Teledyne Brown in Huntsville, Alabama, and repeat the process, and then on to Teledyne Allvac in Monroe, North Carolina, and so on.

It was a very efficient way to stay in touch, and always refreshing for me to visit the management offices and factories that made up Teledyne. I believe people will tell you things in person that they would likely not tell you if you weren't there. Another life lesson.

EXECUTIVE OF THE YEAR AWARD

In September of 1995, I was selected for a national award. My "Executive of the Year" was sponsored by the National Management Association. Again, on the recommendation of both the Ryan Management Associations. It was an honor and privilege. My family and a number of my company presidents flew down to Houston for the festivities.

George Roberts, me and Bill Rutledge at the corporate office on my birthday in the mid 90's.

BLINDSIDED

In the old days, I would walk out in the plant and look for problems. In my corporate job, I didn't have to do that, all I had to do was wait for the phone to ring!

One day Jim McGovern, the President of Teledyne Brown Engineering, called me. Jim was a Naval Academy graduate, fighter pilot, a lawyer and worked as a congressional staffer on the Hill in Washington, D.C. before joining Teledyne.

First, he managed the Washington Office. Then I made him the President of Teledyne Brown, in Huntsville, Alabama. I was taken aback when Jim bluntly advised me by phone that he had filed suit against the Boeing Company for breach of contract. He said that the Teledyne Brown contract with Boeing for Space Shuttle software called for integrating among other things, all the experiments aboard.

The contract required Boeing to give Brown 20% of their NASA contract's value. Jim said that his company had only received around 9% over a period of years.

How could he make such a move without consulting me? He hadn't even made me aware of the problem in the first place!

The Boeing Company was a big customer of Teledyne Companies for many, many products and services. Boeing would react. When one of their suppliers files a lawsuit against them, the company almost automatically shuts down all their contracts with any associated divisions of the threatening company. Contract suspensions were certainly coming for each of my companies that had business with Boeing. I could almost hear the company president's complaints already. The "fat was in the fire."

A POOR DECISION

Jim said he called the President of Boeing and told him of his complaint. He had demanded action or he would file. I knew the CEO of Boeing. His name was Frank Shrontz, and we were friends from the Conquistadors. Frank was a lawyer, a solid businessman, respected in the industry, and had been a friend of mine for years. For sure, he was not the kind of man you would get anywhere with "threats."

I told Jim that he had no business in launching a law suit on his own, and, he had taken away the opportunity for someone else to try and resolve the issue without resorting to the courts.

Indeed, all our contracts with Boeing were put on "indefinite hold."

To make a long story short, there was an "arbitration clause" in the contract, and that is what came next. Jim was out of it, so Terry and I would represent Teledyne Brown Engineering versus The Boeing Company. David, meet your Goliath! To the best of my recollection, we spent the next six months making our case to the arbitrator in a number of meetings in various cities. Concurrently, we were negotiating with Boeing to find common grounds to settle. My opponent was the General Counsel of Boeing.

At the Portland, Oregon meeting, an agreement was finally reached wherein Boeing would provide $125M of new work value to Brown, a good ending! This issue consumed virtually all of my time for six months, not to mention its impact on my key lieutenant, Terry. It was a major distraction, and negatively impacted Profit Plans of a number of Teledyne Companies, both A&E and SM. The entire thing was infinitely preventable.

Looking back, perhaps I should have released Jim immediately, but I knew if I had, it would have given Boeing another card to play with the arbitrator. By the time it was over, I was so relieved that I forgot how mad I was at Jim and let it go.

UNWELCOME NEWS

In the fall of 1996, Frank Wisner, now the Ambassador to India, invited Joan and I to come and visit hIm and his wife for a week in

India. Frank, you may recall, was our Ambassador to Egypt when we worked closely together on the SCARAB licensing issue, and became friends. We were delighted to accept, and started making arrangements.

About a week before we were to leave, Joan mentioned she was having "potty" problems. I told her to see a doctor. I didn't want her going to India with any intestinal problems! She made an appointment to see the doctor and called me. The problem was a tumor in her colon, which would require surgery. I cancelled our trip and arranged for her surgery with her Oncology Team. It would be at the Pomerado Hospital in Poway, just minutes from our home in Rancho Bernardo.

Howard came down from Los Angeles to be with me, and we waited together for the surgeon to tell us the results. He met with us and said that the surgery went well. He had removed about a four-inch section of her intestine. However, when he was in there he looked at her liver, and it was covered with tumors! Her cancer had metastasized from breast, to bone, to liver.

I said, "Well, cut them out."

"You don't understand," the doctor said. "It would be impossible to do that. I'm sorry."

I was dumbstruck. Joan had fought cancer for 19 years. She was Dr. Just's longest surviving patient. She had fought it hard and successfully, and I could not imagine that we couldn't overcome it this time as well. When she was discharged from the hospital, we went to see her oncologist, Dr. Just. He put up an x-ray of her liver. No one had anything to say.

Joan was stoic, as always. We returned every two weeks or so to see Dr. Just, but there was nothing really to be done. She was failing. In February 1997, I went to the company and told them that I was going home to take care of Joan. I did. In May, we went to see Dr. Just.

"Are you sure there is nothing you can do for me?" Joan asked. The doctor started to say no, but stopped himself.

THE COCKTAIL

"Well, I suppose we could make up a cocktail, but it would be a very long shot."

I suggested that we take a trip, "Anywhere you want, and enjoy our time together."

"No." Joan said, "Give me the cocktail." They administered the cocktail by IV. Shortly thereafter, she went into a coma, and I called hospice. We sat in the bedroom with her for a week. She was comatose. Joan passed away in the late morning of Memorial Day, 1997.

The emptiness I felt in losing her was indescribable.

We were both just 14 years of age when we met at Alhambra High School. We dated for eight years through high school and college, and were married for 40 more years, a virtual lifetime.

Joan was from solid Norwegian and Swedish stock; her parents were from Wisconsin. She was strong-willed, and emotionally tough, not a whiner in any sense of the word. In spite of her time being cut short, she lived a happy life. She loved her family and friends, and gave generously of her time to worthy causes. We supported each other over some rough spots in life. She was a full partner in everything we did, from raising the boys, and picking avocados, to managing our apartment complex.

JOAN

Fortunately, she lived long enough to enjoy many of the successes of "Our Life." She saw the boys get married and have children, among other things. We had spectacular trips together around the world, and met many interesting people. We also made several visits to Norway and Sweden so she could experience and enjoy her heritage.

She was a 19-year cancer patient, which tells you a lot about her strength of character. No one knows how she did that. She didn't give up when she lost her breast, nor when she suffered through radiation. She was tough when the cancer destroyed her femur, and then part of her intestines, finally landing in her liver. She bore her pain and fears without complaint. Joan taught me a great deal about living your life fully, and when it comes, meeting death with calm and dignity. I was her partner on the long journey from diagnosis in 1978, to holding her hand in 1997 as she left us. Neither of us would have had it any other way.

The Paris Air Show was coming up, and I went back to the office. I had to attend the show, and stayed at the Hotel Crillon in a suite long reserved for Joan and me. It was really sad. At the Chalet, everyone was very supportive. I did my best to "carry on." But, I knew that I was in trouble. I came home and realized that I had lost my spark, I was empty. I had no desire or interest. The time had come, and I retired.

THE MERGER

Let me tell you briefly about the merger. Teledyne agreed to merge with Allegheny Ludlum Corporation (AL), a Pittsburgh based manufacturer of stainless steel, which is basically a commodity business.

I don't know for sure, but I believe the deal was driven by Henry's illness and the desire to "monetize" his significant holdings in Teledyne equities. George was encouraging me to start a new career with the new company, Allegheny Technologies Inc. (ATI). At his urging, I made a number of trips to Pittsburgh to meet with the new ATI president, Richard Simmons. He coveted Teledyne for two primary reasons. One was its overfunded pension plan and the second was its Specialty Metals companies. I don't know if it was his personality, background in commodity stainless steel or what, but he did not understand or grasp the A&E businesses. After many of my explanations over dinner at his club, he never warmed to them, and I didn't warm to him. I had no desire to move to Pittsburgh, and of course, there was Joan's situation to consider.

What I did do was exercise my stock options for 325,000 shares of Teledyne stock. I hoped the sale of those stocks plus my company retirement would allow for a comfortable life of leisure ahead. Teledyne had a lovely retirement party for me at Jimmy's and all my "Troops" were there, plus a number of corporate staff as well. It was an especially memorable evening for me, and after all the years of effort together, I was sorry that Joan wasn't part of it.

Richard Simmons eventually became the CEO of the new company, ATI. That was the end of our troublesome friend Mr. LaBow! Don Rice resigned to pursue other interests, as did Bill Rutledge. I had retired a year earlier after Joan's death so, no principals stayed on with the new company.

I noted earlier that I was always on the lookout for talent in my companies. I was impressed with a young accountant at Teledyne CAE, a turbo jet engine company. His name was Rich Harshman, and In 1989 I brought him to Los Angeles on my staff. He was an excellent addition, and later worked on the COO's staff. After the merger with Allegheny, he opted to join them and rose through the ranks to CEO of Allegheny Teledyne Inc. Rich is another good example of the benefits of identifying and developing talent In your company."There are no limits."

WRAPPING UP

As I mentioned earlier, corporate life at Teledyne was different. I did not feel the connection there that I so enjoyed when I ran my own companies, and I missed it. Yet, corporate had its own appeal. It was the heart of the corporation, responding to the varied needs of its many companies across a broad spectrum of requirements. I enjoyed my senior role in the corporation, attending stockholder meetings and going on the floor of the New York Stock Exchange with the brokerage house, who managed our stock, among other things. It was rewarding to me to be in a position where I could influence my companies and their leadership in what they did and how they did it. I also enjoyed presenting my segment to the board of directors.

Managing company presidents was particularly challenging, and called for patience and sensitivity. Just because you were their "boss" did not buy you their respect. That you had to earn. And I wanted to earn it! I believe that's the best way to manage. Another life lesson. It was easy for me to identify with them, for I had been "one of them." I could understand and appreciate their concerns and fears, because I had been there too. Although some of my presidents were more forthcoming than others, I established an atmosphere that could not only sustain, but encourage open and frank views and opinions. No games, no B.S.

In some ways, it was harder dealing with the egos of some of my associates at the Corporate office, and their interest in political gamesmanship. I found it difficult to abide those small, insecure men. There were a number of talented people at Corporate: Rich Harshman, Doug Grant in Finance, Dan Lukasik and Nancy McGinnis in HR, among others.

A lady I enjoyed and highly respected was Judith Nelson, our General Counsel. I would stop in to see her, not so much for particulars, but just to say hi. She had a dry sense of humor and a quick wit, and I found she had good insights into Teledyne's workings. One of the things I admired about her was her excellent staff. I worked with all of them on a variety of issues. Mary Doyle, Mike Russell, Mark Aspinwall and Josh Zarrow… They were all competent, and a delight to work with.

I hope this chapter has not come across as a negative in my life. The fact that life at Corporate was different is not a bad thing in and of itself. It is just a different path in the pursuit of common business goals than what I was used to.

Of course, I am sorry that my time there coincided with the reduction in defense budgets, the DoD's policy regarding fixed price development contracts, and Operation Ill Wind. Obviously, nothing could be done about those things. Of the issues which negatively affected me, Operation Ill Wind was by far the worst.

All in all, my career was successful beyond my dreams. Interestingly, it made me grow as I went; the higher I went, the higher I raised my sights. Was I sorry not to be the CEO of Teledyne? Damn right!

HINDSIGHT

It took a while for me to realize that there was no way it could have happened, given all the issues. I had little to do with them, but it made no difference in the final analysis. Once I saw the situation through the eyes of others, I finally understood it. Also, looking back on the Thiokol Corporation opportunity, even if Joan had agreed to go and meet the board (and they would have loved her) it was still not a "sure thing" that I would have accepted their offer *at that time.*

As I said earlier, I believed I had a legitimate chance to be CEO of Teledyne, for all the reasons you have read in earlier chapters. If I had not been considered a candidate for succession to the CEO role, I don't believe I would have been brought to the corporate office in the first place. Further, you may recall in Chapter Seven, where I related the requirements to be a Conquistador; "You had to be a CEO, or be in line to be CEO." The board never really had a choice regarding a comparison of Bill's and my abilities, backgrounds, and personalities for CEO. That decision was taken away by events.

Clearly, it would have meant more to me to be the CEO of Teledyne than Thiokol's (with all due respect to Thiokol).

I was only 62 when Joan died. If Teledyne had not merged, and if she had lived, I would have stayed on enjoying a great life with her and the company. As it was, I had 25 good years with Teledyne and 40 with Joan. As Will Rogers once said: "One must wait until evening to see how splendid the day was."

During my corporate career, there were occasions when my country asked me to support sensitive and highly classified operations. They remain classified to this day, but I am proud to simply note that I never once turned down a request to help our country.

CHAPTER TEN

Retirement, Ad Infinitum: July 1997

I am fortunate to have been retired for almost 20 years before writing this book. It might have been different were it 10 years after retirement. I have now had the chance (and maturity) to look back on some wonderful times and some turbulent times in my life and career. I've made some good decisions, and some poor ones, but when it was all said and done, it was a great trip! I was very fortunate to have been able to take it.

Some events in a career are fortuitous, but I believe many can be influenced by one's decisions. The following is an example of what I mean.

One of the things I learned early in my professional life was that there were a lot of "sharp pencils" in the box. At Autonetics I met my first serious competitors. There were 30 or so young men in the Contracts, Pricing and Proposals Department. All of them had technical, legal, business, or accounting backgrounds. Many of them were very sharp, and everyone wanted to advance.

With my Economics degree, decent résumé, and interviews I was fortunate enough to land a job on the Chief Engineer's staff. I remained there for a year, followed by two years working in an engineering project office. This experience gave me great technical and political insight. I understood what the company did, how they did it, who did what, and how it all fit together. In addition to building a solid foundation at the company, it gave me an edge in knowledge, personal connections, and insights into how the organization worked, and who were the key players.

I believe a good understanding of "your company" is vital, regardless of what business you are in. Another life lesson.

The next step was more difficult. Whether you were administering a contract such as the Minuteman Missile Program, pricing/estimating contracts on existing programs or working on proposals, it was vital to differentiate yourself from the competition. Being creative is one way to distinguish yourself. It doesn't need to be earth-shaking, just different. I was in new business proposals and we were competing with the best in the industry: IBM, General Dynamics, Republic Aircraft, and Lockheed, among others. I reviewed the proposals my company had been submitting and found them to be boring!

Perhaps no one remembers mimeograph ditto machines and elementary printing capabilities, but that's what we had in those days. One idea I had was to put covers on our proposals. Not only covers, but colored ones! That quickly became standard practice. I also found that subtle things contributed to my success. I fought to get Ruth Ehrlic, my secretary, one of the first IBM Selectric Typewriters in the department. It was a big deal at the time.

I worked especially hard on writing a well thought out proposal transmittal letter to the customer for signature by our president.

In addition, I started what became company-wide policy: to write and include an Executive Summary in all technical and management proposals.

All this helped me to be selected as the Major Systems Proposal Coordinator in the new Systems Division. As you may recall, that led to my becoming a line manager, and I was on my way! Another life lesson.

A SORRY SALE

When I retired from Allegheny Teledyne Inc. (ATI), I told the president and CFO that if they decided to sell any of my companies, to please call me first, as I was going to work with a firm that buys and operates these kinds of companies.

"Absolutely, Hudson, you're on the top of the pile." They assured me.

In less than a year, unfortunately, they sold TRA to Northrop Grumman. I understand if ATI management felt that TRA was not a good fit for them going forward. It's also possible they believed the business could prosper more in the hands of a prime contractor like Northrop Grumman... but $140M for a company which today, 16 years later, still has a backlog over $1B? Nonsense!

MAKING A DIFFERENCE

During Joan's last days, I determined to do something for her. I thought about several things, but settled on an endowment for cancer research. I interviewed the Cancer Centers at Stanford, USC, and UCLA. I decided on the Johnsson Comprehensive Cancer Center at UCLA as the most promising. Dr. Judy Gasson was the Director of the Center. When we met, her optimism and strength of purpose came through. Her researchers were developing a new treatment for cancer, one that just killed cancer cells, not everything else. I was impressed by their program, and opened the Joan J. Drake Endowment for Excellence in Cancer Research. I also joined the board, and served six years, making additional contributions to the endowment along the way. It was a wonderfully comforting thing, and I enjoy it to this day.

LA JOLLA

Being at home in Rancho Bernardo, it did not take long for me to realize that I could not continue to live in the house Joan and I had shared for 25 years. Though the market was down, I put it up for sale, sold it, and received a fair price. Joan and I had scouted La Jolla as the next place to live when we retired. I renewed the search and found a condo on Coast Boulevard, immediately across the street from the famous La Jolla Cove.

It was a two bedroom, two bath condo on the third floor of a five story condominium. Each condo took up the whole floor, and the elevator (equipped with your own key) opened right into your unit. It had a large deck with spectacular views of the cove, the ocean, and the coast all the way up to Oceanside. I bought it in the fall of 1997, and immediately hired a decorator to start a major remodel.

I moved in January 1998. It was delightful!

***Howard, me and Paul across the street from my new condo,
La Jolla, 1998***

In La Jolla I affiliated with the local Episcopal Church, St. James by the Sea. I spent many hours in the chapel with my tears. I did get better. As they say, "Time heals all wounds." I joined the Vestry and served a three year term as Investment Chair. I also became a Reader and Intercesssor, and serve to this day.

In one of my first efforts to re-start my life, I applied for a membership at the La Jolla Country Club. It was a beautiful, private club established in 1927 very close to the La Jolla village. I went through the application process and was duly approved for an equity membership.

However, there was a wait list for equity memberships. The club only allowed 420 equity members, so you had to wait until someone resigned or died to get in. Eventually, my turn came and I received my equity membership. It was a good decision. I had not played golf in years, but got out on the range with a pro and took lessons. I never played enough to be good, but I could hit a long drive and had years of fun playing and socializing with my many dear friends there.

CONSULTING

Del Smith was a Conquistador and we met at one of the meetings. When I retired from Teledyne in 1997, he knew of my background and asked me to help him get his company, Evergreen Aviation, into the Unmanned Air Vehicle (UAV)/drone business. I agreed, and signed on as a consultant. I worked with Del for seven years.

Evergreen is headquartered in McMinnville, Oregon, right in the heart of the Willamette Valley wine country! It owned a freight airline of 747s under contract with the Defense Department to supply our forces in the Middle East. Rather than flying back empty after delivering their cargo, the planes would fly on to Asia where they would pick up commercial freight for delivery to the States. In addition, the company ran a fleet of helicopters on a variety of missions, such as flying crews out to oil rigs in the Gulf of Mexico.

I found a small company on the banks of the Columbia River named Insitu. They made an interesting rear engine-mounted UAV that could be launched *and* recovered on land or sea. It was named the Scan Eagle, and had the capacity for a decent payload, loiter time, and altitude. We bought six with support equipment and contracted them out for missions ranging from pipeline inspections to whale surveys in the Gulf of Alaska.

The UAV was good enough, that Insitu was purchased by Boeing several years later!

Del had also put a lot of money into developing a tanker for fighting forest fires. His analysis showed that insurance companies and the U.S. Forestry Service could save money by having his tankers available to fight fires in a timely and efficient way. Del took one of his Boeing 747-200s and developed a system that could be rolled on and off the aircraft as needed. It consisted of pressurized stainless steel tanks holding 22,000 gallons of retardant. The retardant could be released through four nozzles in the aft section of the aircraft. The system was digital and pressurized, so it could release a full or partial load precisely, as opposed to the then current tankers, which relied on gravity to drop their entire load at one time.

Unfortunately, neither insurance companies nor the Forestry Service were interested in supporting the tanker between fires. There was no sale, his benefit analysis notwithstanding.

AN INITIATIVE

Considering the Chernobyl cloud, I had the idea that a large payload UAV tanker such as Del's 747 could be used to "knock down" the toxic cloud formed by an activated nuclear weapon. Once an analysis was done on the weapon's chemical content, counter measures could be quickly loaded in pre-placed tankers and dispatched to slow/stop the cloud from forming or traveling to neighboring states and countries. This could prevent the significant environmental damage and loss of life suffered by the Western USSR and Europe in 1986.

My plan faltered, however. Difficulties arose regarding access to the 747 flight control box. That was necessary in order to modify the aircraft flight control system so it could fly unmanned through the toxic clouds to disperse the chemicals and knock down the cloud. There was also a lack of interest in some quarters on the premise that a defense would be unnecessary due to "mutually assured destruction." I hope they're right, but I still worry about "dirty bombs." They could be set off virtually anywhere and we would have no prompt defensive counter.

SOCIAL LIFE

Sometime after Joan's death, several good friends took it upon themselves to introduce me to some very nice women. I invited several of them out to dinner on separate occasions. While I enjoyed the conversations and the evenings, I just wasn't ready yet. Several months later, I met a lady from Solana Beach. We dated for a period of time. Then in December of 1998, I met Mary. This is a little complicated, but interesting.

When I was President of the Aerospace and Electronics Segment of Teledyne, one of my companies was Aircraft Products, which was based in Mobile, Alabama. Under the name of Continental, it manufactured and sold piston engines to airplane manufacturers such as Piper Aircraft in Vero Beach, Florida. Piper owed us $5M for engines, but was in bankruptcy. The only way we were going to get our money back was to bring them out of bankruptcy and get them up on their feet.

Which we did. I joined the board along with the President of Aircraft Products, Bryan Lewis. In addition, the bankruptcy court appointed a board member, Barbara Barrett, an experienced avaitrix. Her husband was Craig Barrett, CEO of the Intel Corporation at the time.

The Barretts lived in the Phoenix area, and Barbara flew commercially to Vero Beach, via a stopover in Atlanta, for board meetings. I flew commercially as well, from Los Angeles to Atlanta, and then arranged for a company Cessna II aircraft to pick me up and take me to Vero Beach. This was very convenient!

When I became aware of Barbara's travel difficulties, I invited her to fly with me from Vero Beach directly to Atlanta where she could make connections to Phoenix. I would do the same for Los Angeles. We had many interesting discussions on our flights, and soon became friends. I learned Barbara and Craig owned a lovely fishing lodge on the Bitterroot River in Darby, Montana. Barbara ran it. Howard and I had a great trip there.

AN INVITATION

Perhaps a year or so later, I received an invitation from her inviting me and three guests to a black tie dinner at the Beverly Wilshire Hotel in Beverly Hills, honoring Barbara as "Woman of the Year." The gala was sponsored by the Executive Women in Hospitality organization. It held an annual competition for women involved in the hospitality industry. The chair of each state selected a woman as the state's representative in the competition. The Arizona state chair was Mary Vaugier. She selected Barbara Barrett...who won!

MEETING MARY

As they lived close by, I invited Howard and his wife, Susan, to join me. I also invited a lady I knew in Los Angeles. We arrived at the hotel where we were part of some 600 odd guests. I saw a striking woman standing on the grand staircase to the mezzanine. That was Mary. She was monitoring who could go up for the private champagne reception for the honoree, Barbara. She smiled as we passed. Wow! She was beautiful!

She had a great smile, short salt-and-pepper hair, and a svelte body fitted into a sleek green velvet gown! Oh my!

I also happened to notice she wasn't wearing a wedding ring...

As the evening progressed, I made sure we had a chance to talk. My date, who was also in the business, wanted to meet Mary as well. Mary gave her a card. I got one too, but I could have also gotten her information from Barbara.

Playing it cool, I waited a week or so before I used the number on her card to phone Mary at her office in Paradise Valley, Arizona. I got a recording and left a message saying who I was, where we had met, and asking her to call me. She returned my call and we talked for a while. I asked if I could come and take her to lunch or dinner sometime before Christmas.

"Well, that would be nice," she said. "but, I can't do it until late January."

I thought, *uh, oh!* But said, "Fine." and we set a date. I flew to Phoenix on the appropriate date, and she met me at the gate... this was back in the old days!

FIRST DATE

We went to lunch at Lon's at the Hermosa and had a get acquaint-ed-type conversation. I told her about my life, and she told me about hers. She was born in Havana, Cuba to a Spanish mother and Cuban father. She had a business and was divorced with an adult daughter named Nicole. They lived in Paradise Valley.

We had cocktails and meals together for the rest of the weekend... and lots of conversation. On Sunday, she picked me up from the hotel and took me to the airport. All in all, a very exciting weekend for me.

I made another date to see her. I also sent her three dozen, long-stemmed yellow roses with a note thanking her for a lovely weekend. Another life lesson.

I must admit, I was quite taken with Mary. For the first time since Joan's death, I felt alive again. Could I be lucky enough to have found another wonderful woman? I flew to see her at every opportunity. The more time I spent with her, the more certain I was that this was a woman I would be happy with.

On Mary's first visit to La Jolla, I planned to take her to a popular local restaurant in the village, Le Tapenade. The day before she arrived, I went to the restaurant to check out and select the best table for our dinner. There was a nice window table for two that I liked, but knowing that it was a romantic dinner the young French maître d' said, "No, no! Take the table in the corner, Monsieur. You will touch knees!"

I took the table he recommended, and we did touch knees!

CLOSING THE DEAL

Mary and I dated for a year, traveling between La Jolla and Paradise Valley. We also went salmon fishing in the Queen Charlotte Islands, off the coast of British Columbia, and drove up to the Hotel Bel Air in Beverly Hills for delightful weekends. One night, back in Arizona, I took her to dinner at the first restaurant we had dinner at, Lon's at the Hermosa.

I was very nervous. Mary picked up on it, and asked me if there was a problem. "No, no," I said. "Everything is just fine."

Actually, I had bought her a diamond engagement ring several months before, and on this trip I brought it with me. It was at that moment burning a hole in my pocket. I proposed and she accepted with a big smile and a kiss. I was a very happy man! When I married Mary, she came with a big "good old boy" Golden Retriever named Wyatt. A terrific dog! You'll hear more about him later.

THE QE-2

As my 65th birthday approached, I started to think *what would be new and fun*? I had heard that cruise ships were fun. The only cruising I had done thus far was courtesy of the Navy, and far from a vacation! I looked into it and found an attractive cruise from New York to South Hampton, England, and then on to the Mediterranean Sea.

I called Mary.

"Would you like to join me on a three week, 65th birthday, trans-Atlantic cruise aboard the Queen Elizabeth 2, in the Queen Anne Suite?" I queried. She was delighted.

We flew to New York and boarded the ship. We were taken to our suite and introduced to our butler! It was a lovely suite, boasting a private deck equipped with lounge chairs and a table looking out over the port side of the ship on deck nine. It had a big queen-sized bed, full bath, TV, stereo, bar, and living room with large sliding glass doors to the deck.

Enjoying our deck on the QE-2, 2000

There is nothing democratic about the QE-2. It is divided into three distinct sections for passengers and there is no way for anyone to sneak into another section. We were in the Queen's Grill section, which was the equivalent of first class. Then there was the Princess Grill, call it business class. Finally, there was the Britannia Club, call it tourist class. The food and service were indeed world class in the Queen's Grill. If you didn't see what you wanted on the day's menu, all you need do is ask your waiter.

CRUISING

Mary and I were having dinner one night at our table, and I noticed that a table nearby was enjoying crab legs, a favorite of mine. It was not on the menu. I asked the waiter about it, and he said, "Oh, if you would like crab legs, Sir, I will have them for you tomorrow." You could ask for salmon, halibut, Rack of lamb or a filet mignon, it made no difference.

We loved cruising! We enjoyed being at sea and getting into the rhythm of life aboard a luxury ship. Typically, we would have breakfast served in our suite or on our deck. Then we would walk laps around the ship on the bleached white oak main deck, two miles or so. Usually, the next thing we did was shower and then have a massage. Then, if your timing was good, it was time for "Team Trivia," then a glass of wine and lunch. After lunch it was nap time followed by a dip in the pool (or relaxing around the pool with a good book). When we were ready, we would head back to our suite, clean up, and prepare for cocktails and dinner. After that, perhaps we would go to the Casino, or a live show in the theater, or dance to a band in the ballroom. Pretty nice duty!

We would only take a cruise if it was at least 50% or more of the time at sea. Stopping every day at some port or other was not our idea of "cruising." Our favorites were Trans-Atlantic, or Trans-Pacific, because there were many days at sea. We took cruises to Japan, Australia, New Zealand, Hong Kong, Barcelona, Lisbon, and Athens. They typically lasted 30 days or more, and were thoroughly enjoyable.

Mary and I in Venice, 1999

PROSTATE CANCER

Throughout my life I was always good about having an annual physical. I was in the Executive Program at the Scripps Clinic in La Jolla for years. One year, my internist referred me to a urologist because he felt my prostate specific antigen (PSA) was getting too high at about 4.2. The urologist biopsied my prostate (3 "sticks") and found nothing.

He repeated the process six months later, with the same results. He told me to come back in six months. I thought to myself, *Hudson, you're on the board of the Johnsson Comprehensive Cancer Center at UCLA...hello?* I called Judy Gasson and she set me up to meet the chairman of the urology department, Dr. Jean de Kernian. He did 12 biopsies across my prostate and found cancer! It was not a eureka moment for me!

He said, "Look, Hudson, you're 65. If you were 55, I would insist on surgery. If you were 75, I would say, forget it. But at 65 you have to make a call."

There are two well-known drawbacks to prostate surgery. One is incontinence, the second is the inability to function sexually.

Dr. de Kernian said, "I do not have incontinent patients."

Good news there, I thought. He told me about half his patients had no difficulty sexually, and there are things to help the other half. Mary and I talked it over, but it wasn't much of a discussion. We voted for life and a future. I would have the surgery.

I told the doctor of our decision and asked when he could schedule it. We had a cruise coming up, and I wanted to know if we should change our plans.

"No problem," he said, "I couldn't take you before your return anyway."

So, we went.

When we returned, I had the surgery at UCLA, and everything went well. He did tell us that after they sectioned my prostate, they found cancer at both ends of the gland!

I had the old-fashioned, intrusive surgery: opened from navel to pubic bone. Today, most of these surgeries are done through a laparoscope, which is much less intrusive.

Happily, I have been cancer free for 17 years… and counting!

Any time you are told that you have cancer, it's a shock. I thought my family had suffered more than its share of cancer, and that I might be spared. My mom had a double mastectomy, my sister had breast cancer and died at 39. My brother died at 59 with undiagnosed prostate cancer, and I had lost Joan to breast cancer at 62.

Needless to say, I was happy that I had established the Cancer Research Endowment at UCLA.

A FAST TRIP TO PARIS

Mary wanted to go to Chanel in Paris to pick out her wedding dress. That sounded like fun to me, so off we went. We had reservations at the Meurice Hotel. I went along with her to Chanel, a lovely place indeed! Mary told them what she wanted, and they showed us to the proper floor. The sales woman, very well-coifed, seated me in a comfortable chair and brought me a glass of champagne.

Mary told the sales woman that the dress could not be white.

She said, "Madame, you can wear whatever you like!"

She tried on several and I shook my head. Then she came out in a long white dress. When she saw the look on my face she said, "This is it." Mary hand-carried the dress home. I must say, she looked spectacular in that dress!

We married, on November 1, 2000 in the chapel at St. James by the Sea in La Jolla. Immediately afterward, we had a reception and dinner at the La Jolla Country Club with some of our closest friends and family. It was very special.

For our honeymoon, we flew to Peru and boarded a small cruise ship for a trip down the Amazon River to Brazil and back. In the evening, everyone would gather on the top deck bar for drinks and conversation. There we met Judy and Tom Thompson, a wonderful couple from Rancho Santa Fe, just up the interstate from La Jolla! We enjoyed dinner together several times.

After dinner one night, I told Mary that I thought Tom had something on his mind. Sure enough, the next evening he informed us that he and Judy were leading a trip to Africa. One of the couples had just dropped out, and he wanted to know if we would like to join them? We looked at each other and said, "Sure! Sounds great!"

Over the next five years or so, we made six trips to various parts of Africa with Tom and Judy. We visited South Africa, Botswana,

Kenya, Tanzania, Zambia, Namibia, and Mozambique. They were really marvelous trips! I bought a 35mm Nikon and a 300mm lens to capture all the beauty and excitement of the continent that I could. I took many pictures, mostly of animals. Some of them were really good! We framed the best ones and hung them in our den.

Speaking of pictures, on one trip we were staying in Botswana in a lovely lodge setting. The lodges we stayed at were delightful, but rustic. Each had most of the comforts of home. Our hut had a private outdoor shower overlooking a beautiful, verdant valley. We decided to take pictures of our unique outdoor shower adventure. We took great care to "frame" the pictures so as to provide for privacy.

When we got home, we took the film to Costco for development and prints. We picked them up and took them home to look at them. Sitting down to review them, we got to the shower pictures. OMG! They were pretty racy! So much for framing our pictures through the camera lens window. I must say, however, that my pictures of Mary were stunning!

***Ready for a spectacular balloon ride
over the Namibian Desert, 2001***

Interspersed with the African trips, the four of us went to Europe. In Paris, we stayed at the Meurice Hotel, and had the pleasure of watching the end of the Tour de France bicycle race from a re-served area in front of hotel. The racers went around the Place de Concorde several times in celebration of the end of the race, which was won by Lance Armstrong. Quite a colorful spectacle!

We then flew to Switzerland and drove to Lake Garda in northern Italy. We spent a week at the lovely and historic Grand Hotel a Villa Feltrinelli, bordering the lake. The hotel was built by an old lumber family, and the interior woodwork was absolutely lovely! The rooms, food, and service were 5-Star! One evening we had the hotel drive us to Verona for an outdoor spectacular...Aida, performed in an amphitheater. Magnificent! Another day we went to Lake Como and stayed at the Bellagio Hotel. Lunch by the lake was absolutely beautiful.

THE CANAL DU MIDI

Finally, we drove south to Marseille, France. We took a five-day cruise on the Canal du Midi from Marseille to Carcassonne. The canal was completed in 1691, during the reign of Louis XIV. It is one of the oldest canals still in operation in Europe and plays a key role in connecting the Mediterranean with the Atlantic.

We had arranged for the rental of a luxury river barge for just the four of us! The barge, named the "Clair de Lune," had a crew of seven including a fabulous chef. It was a delightful experience! We stopped each day at villages and bought fresh local French foods like bread, cheeses, and wine. The landscape was beautiful and we thoroughly enjoyed relaxing on comfortable deck chairs with a glass of wine as we slowly worked our way through the countryside and canal locks to Carcassonne.

THE FERRARI

I owned and loved a beautiful 1996 Porsche S Carrera, which I drove for several years. But I always hankered for a Ferrari!

I decided to buy one, a 1998 Ferrari 355 GT from the Beverly Hills Ferrari dealership. Of course it was red! It was also one of only 23 in the entire U.S. It was a fantastic car. Everything you could want--style, beauty, handling, power and the unique sound of Ferrari's V-8 engine! I was careful where I drove it. It was clearly not an everyday driver. You didn't just take it to the market or hardware store in the village.

We joined the local Ferrari Club, and took drives with the group to fun places like Hearst Castle and other great road venues.

Mary and I by my Ferrari at a club event, 1999

Following our wedding in November, we returned from our honeymoon in December and found ourselves with no Christmas Tree or other visible signs of the season in the house. I suggested that we make reservations at the Ritz Carlton in Dana Point, about an hour or so up the interstate. It was a very nice hotel, located right on the coast. I told Mary that when I was working I invited my company presidents and their wives to the Ritz for a celebration and wonderful dinner each Christmas. The hotel was always beautifully decorated and carolers walked about the hotel singing all the seasonal favorites. Mary thought it a great idea.

She reminded me that we would have to board Wyatt, but she knew a kennel which was right on our way. Would it be OK to take Wyatt in the Ferrari? I said, "Sure, but he will have to sit on your lap." Wyatt weighed 65 lbs. and by the time we got to the boarding facility Mary was certainly ready to get him off her lap. His nose also made unique designs on the car window! At any rate, we checked him in for the weekend.

We arrived at the Ritz, and the head valet took the car. He told us he would park it with the other "high end" cars, and the keys would be locked up. He told us that he needed the keys in the event of an emergency or if the night crew needed to steam clean the driveway.

We enjoyed a lovely dinner and retired to our room for the night. Around 1:00 A.M., the phone rang. We were told that there had been an accident with our car, and would we please come to the front?

Mary asked, "What is it, did someone back into it?"

"No," she was told, "you need to come to the hotel entrance."

We sleepily complied. When we got there, there were a number of employees standing around, but no car.

"What's the problem," I asked. "Where is my car?"

The valet pointed down the driveway. There was another crowd some ways down, and you could see a headlight. Mary and I walked down the drive. There was our Ferrari, well off the driveway and on the grass, jammed into a big palm tree! The front of the car was demolished. It seems that a young valet had been quite taken by the car. When his shift ended at midnight, he broke into the locked key box. He took one of his friends for a ride, and then returned to take another friend out.

OH NO!

Needless to say, Ferrari's are extremely powerful. The acceleration is something to behold. The car got away from him speeding down the driveway, jumped the curb and *flew* nine feet over the grass into the tree! Both occupants survived, shaken but unhurt. It was really painful, standing there looking at my smashed dream.

The next day, the hotel drove us home to La Jolla. We picked Wyatt up on the way. The car was taken to the Ferrari dealership where they assessed the damage. Unfortunately, the frame was bent, so the car was pronounced "Totaled." Word of the accident spread, and we were deluged with calls from the press for interviews, ranging from the Los Angeles Times, Orange County Register and Wall St Journal, to the Road and Track Magazine. I didn't see anything to gain by granting interviews so we declined them.

The Ritz, of course, was very sorry. They turned the matter over to their insurance carrier, the Zurich Company. After a few days, their representative called and said the company was prepared to offer us $60,000 for the totaled Ferrari. I told the agent she was nuts! I had paid $185,000 for the car just three years ago, and it had been one of only 23 in the country! It was in perfect condition and had only been driven 10,000 miles. We went back and forth for several months. I finally retained an attorney. When it was all said and done, Zurich reimbursed me what I had paid for the car, and the Ritz paid for my attorney!

Ferrari, in the meantime, had come out with a new model, the 360, since I had bought mine. I called the dealership, which was well aware of the crash, and asked what they could do for me regarding a new car. They advised me that they would put me on the wait-list… which was approximately a two year wait!

I said, "Forget it!" and bought a ladder of municipal bonds instead!

THE BEACH CLUB

In addition to the La Jolla Country Club, where I served on the board of directors for three years as Membership Chair, we decided to join the La Jolla Beach and Tennis Club. It was a mere ten minutes from home. An old, private club, it has tennis courts, a nine-hole pitch and putt course, and an Olympic-sized pool. Its main feature is about 300 yards of ocean front. The beach is raked daily. Towels, chairs, tables and umbrellas are available for the asking from a dutiful staff member, not to mention food and drink.

It is a wonderful place to relax, swim, read or just work on your tan. It is also a fabulous place to have a beach BBQ, and watch the sun sink slowly into the Pacific Ocean with a favorite cocktail in your hand!

HOUSE HUNTING

In 2003, Mary and I decided that the condo wasn't big enough. We put it on the market and started looking for a house in La Jolla. After scouting 20 or so locations, we just hadn't found anything we liked.

Mary did find an old Spanish-style home built in the 1920s. It needed work, but sat on a large deep lot than ran from the street in front of the house to the street behind the house. It was a north-facing two-story with two bedrooms and two bathrooms, and had a lovely view of the ocean and the coast running up north toward Del Mar. The price was right, so we bought it. We did well with selling the condo too.

In many ways, we hated leaving the condo with its ocean ambiance and spectacular views. One of our fondest memories there was the marriage of Mary's daughter, Nicole, to Leandro Velazquez in 2002. The wedding was held on our deck under a beautiful sky.

At our new home we hired an architect and a builder. We converted the two car garage, which was under the house, into my office with a full bath and French doors. We built a new garage in front of the house, allowing room for a nice patio, planters, and a fountain between my office and the garage. We doubled the size of the master bedroom and bath and installed windowed doors, to allow a beautiful view of the ocean and north coast from our bedroom.

It was a much improved house, and we were very happy with the results.

Leandro, Nicole, Mary and me

THE BIG SEVEN OH!

For my 70th birthday in 2005, Mary and I decided to have a big party at the country club to celebrate. Mary did all the planning. I wanted to reach way back for old friends from many parts of my life, and use my birthday to celebrate them as well. We reserved the entire ball room and veranda area. We hired the Wayne Foster Band…all of it! There were some 12 singers, 10 dancers, and the full orchestra. Foster's Band was legend in La Jolla; simply the best. When they played, you couldn't sit still!

We invited about 120 guests from all walks of my life. Since I had been raised in the greater Los Angeles area, many of them still lived close enough to attend. We set up "period" tables: one table for grammar school, another for high school, then college, friends and neighbors, fraternity brothers. From my work years there were tables for Teledyne Ryan Electronics and Aeronautical, and another for Corporate. There was a table for White House Fellows, another for friends we had made in La Jolla, and of course, one for family!

During the evening, I walked to each table with a microphone, addressing my guests and reminiscing about our fun times together. It was wonderful!

Carl Bayer read a congratulatory letter from my old friend, Neil Armstrong. Country Club members still talk about the "beat" of the band which could be heard throughout the club. Looking in to see the source they got to see people having the time of their life. The party was going so strong we extended the band an extra hour! Now that is a fantastic memory!

BEWARE THE FLAME!

In 2011, a fire broke out in our garage. It was caused by faulty wiring in Mary's Mercedes SUV. The fire totally destroyed the garage as well as my Porsche. The fire chief told us that if it wasn't for the patio between the garage and my office, the whole house would have gone up in flames! Needless to say, we were grateful for our renovations! We rebuilt the garage, but this time we added a 2nd story for storage. A really fine idea. Now we could organize all our stuff (luggage, fishing equipment, supplies, etc.) in one convenient place.

Mary decided that since we were getting a new garage, we needed a new kitchen too! Makes sense, right? So we did remodel number two, which completed a total re-do of the house. Besides a new kitchen we installed hardwood floors, rebuilt the stairs and built a pantry and guest bath. We enclosed the upper front porch, and put in a large picture window so you could see the ocean from the living room. The results were spectacular!

TEDDY & WYATT

As I mentioned before, Mary and her Golden Retriever, Wyatt, were a package deal! He was a great dog, a sweet old boy.

In 2001, Mary was at a local shopping center which happened to be featuring a "pet adoption" day. Cages of cats and dogs were stacked high in the parking lot. She stopped by a cage with a Siamese-type kitty in it, big blue eyes and all. Of course, she put her finger in the cage to pet the kitty, which proceeded to nuzzle her finger. That did it. Mary promptly bought the kitty, food dish, food, litter box, and an assortment of goodies, and brought it all home. She walked in with all this paraphernalia and announced that we had a kitty!

My first concern was what about Wyatt? Mary said he would not be a problem, and he wasn't. I had never had a cat, but I had one now. I named him Theodore Roosevelt, "Teddy" for short.

Mary had bought a few stuffed mice as toys. I got down on the floor with Teddy, and threw a mouse up onto a stuffed chair. Ted was right on it. I stashed one behind a cushion, Ted burrowed in and got it. We played this game a lot, and both of us thoroughly enjoyed it. I would start the whole thing by giving a "hissss." Teddy's ears would perk up and he would crouch and be ready to go in a flash... waiting only for me throw the mouse.

CHARGE!

One morning in the condo I was watching the stock market on TV, and noticed some movement to my left. Teddy was crouching in his "attack" position. We had large sliding glass doors leading out to the expansive deck overlooking the cove. One of the doors was open about a foot. Standing on the deck was a huge sea gull, and Teddy was lining up to attack it. Sea gulls are large, sturdy birds and I would guess this one weighed a good ten pounds or more. Twice Teddy's weight!

Well, my imagination went wild. I was afraid he would get a hold on the gull and it would take off with him. At some point, Teddy would fall off and drop at least three floors onto the cement below. But Ted wasn't worrying about that. Before I could say or do anything, he charged the gull. It saw him coming. It's first line of defense was to drop a huge poop on the deck while starting its takeoff run. With wings flapping and feathers flying, the gull cleared the three-foot glass wall just ahead of my boy Ted.

I was afraid for him, and proud of him at the same time. Needless to say, in the future we would keep the glass doors closed unless we were right there on the deck. Why was I surprised by his action? His namesake charged San Juan Hill and Teddy charged the seagull… Figures!

We were good buddies. He followed me around like a dog. He was 15 this year (2016). In our new house we had a kitchen table where I would sit in the morning and read the newspapers and drink my coffee. Ted would jump up on the table and tuck into the crook of my arm. It was very touching.

One day I noticed that his nose was running. After a few days I mentioned to Mary that we should take him into the vet's office, as it seemed he had an allergy. We took him in. The short story is that he did not have an allergy, he had cancer! It had eaten a good part of the bone in his nose and was advanced.

To do all the testing, the vet had anesthetized him. Now the vet needed to know if we wanted to wake him up and take him home for the short time he had left, or put him down while he was still out. We were both in tears, but told the vet not to wake him up. We let him go without pain and with dignity. We had Teddy cremated, and he will be spread at sea with me when my time comes. I loved my Ted!

Teddy

Several months later, Mary heard about Siamese like kittens that had been rescued. They were at a local pet store. She picked out a cute female and brought her home as a surprise. I was not really ready for another cat, but got over it quickly enough when I realized what a live wire Tillie was! She fits right in with all of our other pets in the family.

FLY FISHING

After getting involved with fly fishing from my early Conquistador days, I have fly fished all over the world. From the Zambezi River in Zambia, to Argentina, to Chile. From Alaska, to the Ozernaya River (Oz) on the Kamchatka Peninsula in Russia, from Mongolia to New Zealand and Australia, from Canada and the Yukon to New Brunswick. And of course, many places in Oregon, Washington State, Utah, Wyoming, Montana, Colorado and Arizona.

46" Taiman, the largest Salmonoid species in the world, Mongolia, 2005

I would be remiss if I didn't add the many great places we went to in the Caribbean for Bonefish and Tarpon. I have thoroughly enjoyed the experience and met many interesting people in the process.

I love fly fishing because it's time spent with someone you love or a very special friend. You usually stay in a nice lodge with most of the comforts of home (with the exception of Mongolia and Kamchatka). We bring our own single malt and Irish whiskey to enjoy at day's end, and fish on a lovely stream or river under bright blue skies, or clouds for trout or salmon. It is so special! Just you and "them," under the watchful eye of your guide.

19 lb world class Brown Trout, Rio Grande River, Tierra del Fuego, Argentina, 2004

Enjoying a nip in front of my Mongolian Ger after a long day on the river.

The Oz River on the Kamchatka peninsula, Russia. The best Rainbow Trout stream I have ever fished. Here is a typical 28" beauty.

C DEL C

Conquistadores has been a wonderful experience too. The Spring Meeting was open to guests, and I very much enjoyed bringing several of my company presidents and Carl Bayer from our Washington Office. We played golf, socialized with senior members of the aerospace community, and in general had great fun. I made many wonderful friends over the years at Conquistadores, and have thoroughly enjoyed being part of it.

I served on the board of directors 2005 to 2008. I was awarded my "Yellow Jacket," signifying 25-year membership, in 2011. I look forward to attending the Ranch Meeting every year in September. Mary has met a number of Conquistadores and their wives, either in Paris at the Air Show or here in the States at various events. A really fine group of people!

NEIL'S LANDING ON THE MOON

Of all my conversations with Neil Armstrong over the years, my favorite took place at a CdelC Ranch Meeting. We were at Big Creek for a BBQ lunch, and Neil and I were standing by the creek talking. I asked him about the APOLLO 11 Moon landing when he was piloting the Lunar Excursion Module (LEM). The LEM was following the pre-programmed course set by NASA. As It approached the lunar surface, however, the programmed landing spot was littered with boulders, preventing a landing!

I asked, "What were you thinking"? He replied very calmly "I knew we had to take a good look at the planned landing site to make sure we couldn't land there. So, I turned on your (Teledyne Ryan

Electronics) landing radar. When I got "lock" on the first pulse from the radar, I knew we'd be OK."

Neil thought he had burned about 10 to 12 seconds of fuel looking for an alternate landing site. The fuel indicator light was now blinking red, telling him that he was running very low on fuel. He had about 15 seconds to find an alternate site, and the warning light continued counting down...14...13...12 seconds!. The amount of fuel was critical, because if he used more than the planned amount, the LEM would not have enough fuel to get back to the Command Module and they would be stranded on the Moon! He spotted a landing site and put the LEM down. Neil looked at me and said, "No problem, I had six seconds of fuel left!" Two things struck me: one was that he related this very calmly, while I, on the other hand was in a high emotional state!

Neil was one of a kind, a fraternity brother and a great friend.

One more astronaut story. Jim McDivitt, the Commander of APOLLO IX and I were chatting at a CdelC meeting, and I asked him what kind of tests you have to take to become an astronaut? Jim said, "It's very simple really. You have to have an engineering or physical science degree, and be 6' or under. If you clear those hurdles, you go into an interview pool." Now you know!

APOLLO 11's Neil Armstrong and I at a CdelC Ranch Meeting in Wyoming, mid 1990's.

CdelC Fly Casting Winner - 2013

Over the course of my membership, I won a number of competitive events, but I retired the Fly Fishing Award by winning it three times, and becoming a "Champion of Champions." I have won the Fly Casting competition twice, but am still looking for the magic third win!

PETER FARRELL

While we're talking about fly fishing, I want to say a word about Peter. I am fortunate to have many great friends, but one in particular I have had the pleasure of spending time with in my retirement years is Peter Farrell. We joined the La Jolla Country Club at the same time, and that is where we met over 17 years ago.

Peter and I have played golf in many venues and fly fished together in Chile, the Yukon, British Columbia, Alaska, and in Idaho, Wyoming, Montana and the Florida Keys. During these fishing trips, we have perfected the art of consuming excellent single malts and Irish whiskey after a long day on the river. You can't beat the combination of a fine drink and the pleasure of reliving a delightful day!

One of my favorite things that Peter and I do on most Monday nights, is meeting at the Herringbone Restaurant in La Jolla. We enjoy several dozen fresh shucked oysters on the half shell, a fine bottle of Chardonnay, and finish with a Margherita Pizza. Oh, and solve all the world's problems as well!

THE BIG EIGHT OH

In March 2015, Mary arranged two 80th birthday parties for me. The first was at the La Jolla Country Club, and the second was at the Colonial Hotel in La Jolla.

The first party, at the country club, was for La Jolla friends. Everyone dressed in fishing attire, and Mary had the beautiful decorations and cake to match. It was really fun!

The second night was for family. Howard and his wife, Susan, and their daughter Madeline came down from Los Angeles, my nephew David flew in from Dallas, and Paul, his son, Cameron and fiancé Raissa attended. Altogether, a special dinner with everyone, and a chance to catch up on all the family activities.

THE RONALD MCDONALD HOUSE

I just completed a six year term as a Trustee and Vice-Chair of the Ronald McDonald House Charities-San Diego. It was a wonderfully fulfilling experience helping families who had a severly ill son or daughter accross the street at Rady's Children's Hospital. Mary was also involved, and started the successful "ROMP" Gala, which became an annual fund raiser for the House.

Me, grand daughter Tessa and Mary

YOUNGEST SON, PAUL

2016 is still underway at this writing, and it has been another challenging year. In October of 2015, my youngest son, Paul, was diagnosed with prostate cancer. Perhaps his medical team at Kaiser was so engrossed with his cardiovascular problems over the years that they forgot some of the basic health testing for males, such as periodic PSA checks!

Surgery is not an option, so Paul is receiving hormone therapy, which has dramatically reduced his PSA. He is receiving world class care at the nearby Moore's Cancer Center at the University of California at San Diego. Technology has made tremendous strides in cancer research and treatment. We are hopeful that the research community will find methods to mute, and treatments to cure this insidious disease.

Paul has other health complications, which makes everything more difficult. from his numerous doctor visits to his variety of medications. Mary and I both cover Paul's appointments, but Mary has been there for Paul like no one else.

MY HEALTH

I have been very fortunate health-wise. I deal with arthritis, as many my age do, and have been treated for Glaucoma the last several years. I stay fit by working with weights during the week, and walk the hills of La Jolla (at a pace) every day. I am trim, and carry 180 lbs. on a 6' frame (used to be 165 lbs. and 6'1"). Mary and I love to dance too!

CUBA

In February, Mary organized a trip with good friends to Cuba. She was born in Havana; the daughter of a Spanish mother and a Cuban father. She, her brother and their mother were trapped there by the revolution, as Cubans were not allowed to leave the island. Her father had to leave as soon as possible after the revolution started. His life was in danger due to his father's high political profile.

When she was nine, they got out to Florida, but that's a different story. Mary and I visited Cuba in 2008 by flying out of Monterrey, Mexico to Havana for a fun week.

The 2016 trip was partly in Havana, and the rest in the Pinar del Rio area, which is in the middle of the agriculture and tobacco plantations. The scenery was lovely, and everyone enjoyed themselves. It was a delight to get out of the city and see the country side.

We noticed how much had improved since our first trip, in terms of the quality of the hotels, food options, items for sale, and so on. The people themselves are a happy lot. After years of no contact, Mary found her aunt in Havana. She was able to visit her home, which had belonged to Mary's grandfather. He was the President of the Cuban Senate and a publisher before the revolution.

It was a beautiful, large home set in wooded property. Mary played there as a youngster. Interestingly, former President Bautista owned it at one time. The fact that she found the house in the first place was a minor miracle. That her family still resided there made it even more special. Amazing!

HORSES

Mary became interested in horses again about two years ago. She had horses as a youngster and competed successfully in Hunter-Jumper competitions. Marriage and children stopped all that for a number of years, but here in our area many women are involved with horses, especially among her friends in Rancho Santa Fe. Mary very much wanted to ride again. We leased a horse for a while, but when she found Phoebe, she had to have her.

Mary and Phoebe, 2015

Let me tell you, I have never seen her as happy as she is with that horse! She not only rides her every day, but lovingly cares for her maintenance. In her first competition, a combination horse and rider event, she won two blue ribbons! I was very proud of her and she really looked good out there in the ring.

Early in 2016, Mary approached me with an investment idea. She had resumed riding in Rancho Santa Fe. Her trainer is Guillermo Obligado, an Argentine who rode for Argentina in past Olympics. In addition to training and giving lessons, Guillermo and his wife have a business importing potential Grand Prix Jumpers from Europe. He then trains and sells them to a large Grand Prix following in the Rancho Santa Fe and Southern California area.

These are not racehorses, they are jumpers. The Grand Prix Events are truly spectacular! The riders don dressy riding clothes and the horses are beautifully coifed. We have attended several events at the Del Mar Fairgrounds.

The short story is that we partnered with Guillermo. On one of his trips to Europe he bought a beautiful five-year-old German Warmblood mare, Contilou. Her breed is called Oldenburg. He will train her and when she's ready, start her in competitions so she's exposed to buyers. When the horse sells the costs are deducted, and the balance is shared per agreement. I am just the banker! It's up to Guillermo and Mary to make this work! We'll see.

Contilou and Guillermo looking good at the
Del Mar Horse Show, 2016

A SECOND MARRIAGE

I remarked earlier in the book that when I met Mary and spent some time getting to know her, I thought I had found another special woman in my life. I was well aware that second marriages could be difficult, and that the odds of a success might be relatively small. Let me relate the story of our fishing trip to the Queen Charlotte Islands in British Columbia in 1999. It's just one example of how I knew that Mary was the "one."

We helicoptered from the mainland to a ship, named the Salmon Seeker, anchored in Kenoe Inlet. There were about 24 people aboard, including several women.

Our cabin was really small. The bunk beds were angled to allow for the hull, so you slept at about a 100-degree angle. Your slickers hung on hooks in the overhead of the cabin, just over our bunks. Big yellow rubber boots completed the ensemble. The showers and heads were down the passageway. None of this was particularly conducive to romance!

Each morning we would have an early breakfast and be in our whaleboat ready to go by 7:30. It was a cold 45 minute ride out to the fishing grounds. We sat in the stern of the boat with our backs to the wind, snuggled together and holding hands for warmth. It was a special time and neither of us felt it necessary to say anything.

When we arrived at the fishing grounds, our skipper set up our gear and we started fishing for salmon. Whenever one of us landed the first fish, regardless of the hour, we high-fived and had a beer. Sometimes we ate a peanut butter and jelly sandwich as well! We had a wonderful time!

We spent five days and nights together without a cross word between us. Neither of us said or did anything that bothered the other. Our senses of humor were compatible, and we shared our thoughts and feelings easily. Mary was always positive, a good sport, and had a smile on her face. It was a very special time together. I felt that I had gotten to know the "real" Mary, and she was the "one."

Mary and I enjoying our Salmon catch at day's end.

BACK TO WORK!

Mary and I have been friends with Eloisa and Chris Haudenschild for many years. In June 2016, Chris asked me to come to work for him. This request was based on my business experience and our numerous conversations about issues he had at his company. He thought I could help him solve them!

Chris started his business 33 years ago, and it has been an amazing success in the Electronic Health Record (EHR) industry. His company, CliniComp, has the contracts for all 59 of the Department of Defense Medical Treatment Facilities around the world. It also has 37 Veteran Administration hospitals and 20 commercial sites. The company's database holds personal medical information for millions of patients and must be available 24/7 to medical staff... it has a near perfect record!

Chris brought me aboard to advise him in making his organization more responsive and efficient. This has been a whole new world for me. A private company, information technology, intensive software products, new vocabulary and so forth. As this year draws to a close, we have made progress. I have thoroughly enjoyed the challenge and the opportunity!

GRANDCHILDREN

It is probably the goal of all grandparents to see their grandchildren marry. I am fortunate to have four grandchildren and hope to see them all married. I believe I have a good chance at seeing at least two more of them married, the fourth one is only 11... it might be a really long shot, but?

HANNA AND MADELINE DRAKE

On September 17, 2016, my only grandson, Cameron, married a lovely young lady named Raissa Lima. The ceremony was in the Chapel at the St. James by the Sea Church, the same place Mary and I were married 16 years before! The flowers and music were lovely and the smiles on the faces of the bride and groom lit up the entire chapel! The weather was fabulous, as was the wedding party. The ceremony was followed by a reception nearby where the participants and guests enjoyed drinks and dinner under the stars

Me, Raissa, Cameron and Mary at St. James, La Jolla.

I think the beginning of Cameron and Raissa's life together is a fitting place to end this, my life story.

Writing this book made me realize what a wonderful life I have lived, and for which I am truly thankful.

I am hopeful that Mary and I will have continued good health and the enjoyment of our friends and family.

I was just advised that I am to be inducted into the San Diego Air and Space Museum's Hall of Fame on November 9, 2017. Quite an honor, I am thrilled!